Shelf Expression

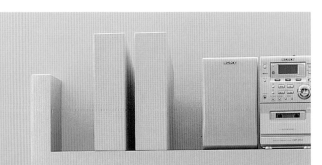

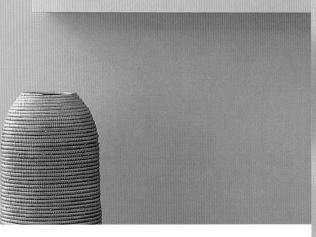

Shelf Expression

70 Projects & Ideas for Creative Storage & Display

Marthe Le Van

LARK BOOKS

A Division of Sterling Publishing Co., Inc.
New York

Art Director: Dana Irwin

Cover Designer: Barbara Zaretsky

Assistant Art Director: Hannes Charen

Production Assistant: Shannon Yokeley

Assistant Editor: Nathalie Mornu

Editorial Assistance: Delores Gosnell

Photographer: keithwright.com

Woodworking Consultant: Pete Roberts

Proofreader: Sherry Hames

Library of Congress Cataloging-in-Publication Data
Le Van, Marthe.
  Shelf expression : 70 projects & ideas for creative storage & display/ Marthe Le Van.— 1st ed.
    p. cm.
  ISBN 1-57990-466-1
  1. Storage in the home. 2. Shelving (Furniture) I. Title.
  TX309.L48 2004
  648'.8—dc21
                              2003011148
10 9 8 7 6 5 4 3 2 1

First Edition
Published by Lark Books, a division of
Sterling Publishing Co., Inc.
387 Park Avenue South, New York, N.Y. 10016

© 2004, Lark Books

Distributed in Canada by Sterling Publishing,
c/o Canadian Manda Group, One Atlantic Ave., Suite 105
Toronto, Ontario, Canada M6K 3E7

Distributed in the U.K. by Guild of Master Craftsman Publications Ltd.
Castle Place, 166 High Street Lewes, East Sussex, England BN7 1XU
Tel: (+ 44) 1273 477374, Fax: (+ 44) 1273 478606
Email: pubs@thegmcgroup.com, Web: www.gmcpublications.com

Distributed in Australia by Capricorn Link (Australia) Pty Ltd., P.O. Box 704, Windsor, NSW 2756 Australia

If you have questions or comments about this book, please contact:
Lark Books
67 Broadway
Asheville, NC 28801
(828) 253-0467

Manufactured in China
All rights reserved
ISBN 1-57990-466-1
Special Photography

Sanoma Syndication: page 117, 94, 150; Julia Bird, page 32; Dennis Brandsma, pages 8, 15,
55, 65, 95, 97, 113, 119, 122, 123, 141; Frank Brandwijk, page 115; Anneke de Leeuk, page 144;
John Dummer, page 105; Hotze Eisma, page 70; Renée Frinking, page 8; Luuk Geertsen,
pages 139, 147; Rene Gonkel, page 125; Paul Grootes, pages 73, 102; Peter Kooijman, pages
27, 107, 149; Louis Lemaire, pages 53, 108, 109; Dolf Olislagers, pages 126, 127, 128, 129;
Harold Pereira, page 35; Paul Steenbakker, page 104; Dolf Straatemeier, pages 34, 100, 135,
137; John van Groenedaal, pages 47, 96, 110, 111, 121, 153, 155; Eric van Lokven, page 67;
George v.d. Wijngaard, page 103; and Hans Zeegers, page 143.

CONTENTS

INTRODUCTION

Shelves have a plain and simple purpose. They hold things. For sensible storage and decorative display, chances are good you could use a lot more shelves in your home. Why settle for the purely practical when you can have something that looks great, too? This book is loaded with uncomplicated ways to create stylish shelves. Whether you want to transform an everyday object into an unconventional shelf, decorate an unfinished shelf, install commercial shelves in imaginative ways, or build a shelf on your own, let this book be your guide to "shelf-expression!"

You'll find a basics chapter packed with all the technical information and helpful advice you need to install a shelf with confidence. Even if you're baffled by hardware, hangers, and hooks, this chapter will quickly and clearly explain their subtle differences and practical applications. Extra hints for finding studs and drilling holes will help to make your shelf project a success.

Commercial shelving elements can be creative and fashionable. To prepare you for using these options, the basics chapter also covers the fundamentals of brackets and boards, with installation instructions and troubleshooting tips. It covers current design trends for ready-made shelves as well, showing you how to customize them to suit your needs.

The first collection of projects, One-of-a-Kind Shelves & Brackets, features everyday objects transformed into shelves. From skateboards to shower totes, drawers to drink crates, these selections are imaginative, attractive, and even amusing. You'll find shelf ideas for every room, helping you to establish a creative and well-designed living environment. Whether it's a red wagon or a watering can, the elements in these projects are easy to find and easy to hang on your wall.

If you want to embellish an unfinished wood shelf, the second collection of projects, Decorating Shelf Surfaces, is full of spectacular examples you'll enjoy making and hanging in your home. Following step-by-step instructions, you can alter a ready-made

shelf with tiles, molding, wallpaper, paper bags, wood ornaments, wire, paint, and even synthetic suede.

The third project group, New Looks & Uses for Commercial Shelves, shows how to work with prefabricated shelves in inventive, advantageous, and engaging ways. This chapter shows how alternative shelf placement and shelf accessories can enhance your home. For example, you can turn a standard floating shelf into a stylish magazine rack with the surprising addition of metal pipe, or create a dynamic kitchen focal point by pasting a panel of pretty wallpaper behind a shelf set.

Prefacing the final collection of projects, Building Simple Shelves, is a woodworking primer. This section covers the fundamental skills you'll need to make a wood shelf from scratch. Easy-to-make shelves can be attractive, contemporary accents for your home. All of the selected projects are fresh new styles and come with detailed step-by-step instructions.

Between the major shelf collections, you'll discover fact-filled special-interest sections to expand your shelf insight. The topics range from cinder-block alternatives to customizing cubes. There's even an overview of the frequently wasted spaces where you could place a shelf. Throughout the book, you'll find sourcing tips for shelf shopping and design ideas to make sensational-looking shelves. With all this information at your fingertips, you're sure to be more "shelf-aware" and "shelf-motivated!"

THE BASICS

What is the essence of a shelf? So as not to stifle your creativity, we'll be as broad-minded as possible with this definition. Basically, a shelf is a surface, typically horizontal, on which objects are displayed or stored. Shelves can be manufactured for the mass market, crafted individually by hand, or be a lovely synthesis of these two states. A shelf can be as simple and predictable as an unfinished wood board or as surprising as a cluster of aluminum paint buckets.

Structurally, there are two types of shelves, those that are hung and those that are freestanding. A wall-hung shelf can have a single surface or a group of linked surfaces. Its mount can be exposed, such as a bracket, or hidden by the shelf for a floating effect. A hung shelf can also be suspended from the ceiling by some sort of rope or chain. A free-standing shelving unit is not mounted; it sits directly on the floor or on a tabletop.

Shelves are the perfect solution for displaying decorative objects and/or generating additional storage in the home (or office, or garage, or gardening shed). They're practical, adaptable, easy to install, and portable. Transforming unexpected objects into shelves yields outstanding decorative results and is simple once you know a little bit about hardware.

Right: Turn a toolbox into a shelf by attaching two ring hangers (see page 50).

HANGING HARDWARE

Commercial shelves and brackets have the distinct advantage of having hardware and hangers built in to their design. To convert ordinary objects into wall-hung shelves, you'll need to take some preparatory steps. The back side of your soon-to-be shelf will help you decide what type of hanging apparatus to use. Here are some common and easily obtainable pieces of hanging hardware. One is sure to fit your needs.

Adjustable Sawtooth Hangers

Sawtooth hangers mount onto the object you wish to hang. They're made from a horizontal strip of steel that's slightly elevated in the middle. There's a nail hole on each of the hanger's flat ends, and the appropriate nails are frequently packaged with the hanger.

The center of the hanger's bottom edge is serrated in a jagged sawtooth pattern, allowing the hanger to be self-leveling.

To use this type of hanger, nail it to the back side of the object you wish to hang, with its sawtooth edge facing down. Position the hanger on the object to hide the nail or other hanger you'll be using as the wall

hardware. Depending on the object's size and weight, use one hanger in the center or two hangers near each edge. After the hanger or hangers are in place, install the wall hardware at a suitable height and width. Slide the sawtooth hanger over the wall hardware. Adjust the object's placement on the serrations as needed to make it level.

Some sawtooth hangers have sharp-pointed protrusions on their flat ends that take the place of nails. Once you position this type of hanger on an object, you simply push it in with your thumbs. For added security, you may wish to lightly tap the hanger with a hammer.

Keyhole Fasteners

Look at the center of a keyhole fastener, also known as a *hanger plate*, and you'll see that it's very aptly named. Its top and bottom holes are round to accept screws; whereas, its middle opening has a more complex shape. Constructed of heavy-duty steel, this fastener attaches flush against the object you wish to hang. It then slides over wall-mounted screw heads or nail heads, providing your shelves with a well-concealed and incredibly strong mount.

Ring Hangers

Ring hangers attach to the back side of the object you wish to hang. They're manufactured with one or more small holes at the bottom through which screws fasten. The opening at the top of a ring hanger may be round, triangular, or square in shape. Some are flat and stationary, while others pivot to different angles. Ring hangers fit over a wall-mounted nail, screw, hook, or picture hanger, or they can be strung with picture wire. Extra heavy-duty ring hangers often support large (and fragile!) mirrors. Ring hangers are a good choice to achieve a flush mount, and they fit well in diverse locations.

Screw Eyes

Screw eyes have a steel shaft with one end formed into a ring and the other threaded and pointed like a screw. They vary greatly in length, from $1/4$ inch to 3 inches (6 mm to 7.6 cm) long and have various *eye*, or ring, diameters. If you wish to hang your shelf by picture wire (like a frame), you'll need to attach two screw eyes to its back side. (Keep in mind that you won't achieve a flush mount using screw eyes. The larger the eye, the more your shelf will protrude from the wall.)

When positioning your screw eyes, plan to conceal the picture wire once it's taut. You can manually install screw eyes into most surfaces; however, you may wish to make small pilot holes for an easy start. Use pliers to tighten the screws as needed. Large screw eyes are also an excellent choice when hanging a suspended shelf from the ceiling or wall.

Picture Wire

Soft, pliable, and very strong, stainless steel picture wire makes a secure hanging cord for shelves. You can buy it at your local home improvement center or at an art supply store, cut to a specific measurement or in convenient prepackaged lengths.

To install picture wire, thread about 4 inches (10.2 cm) of one end through one screw eye or ring hanger. Bend back the wire and tightly coil it around itself. To determine the amount of wire you'll need, hold it up to the center of the shelf at least $1^1/2$ inches (3.8 cm) below the shelf's top edge, and then run the wire back down to the opposite hook or hanger. Add 4 inches (10.2 cm) to this amount, and cut the wire. Insert the loose wire end through the empty screw eye or ring hanger, bend back the extra 4 inches (10.2 cm), and coil. Pull the wire taut to test its strength.

WALL SUPPORT HARDWARE

Once your new shelf is properly prepared, you'll need to securely attach it to the wall on a suitable device. Most often you'll use a simple set of screws or nails to support the shelf's hanging hardware. Other circumstances may call for more specialized devices.

Choosing & Using the Right Screws

What type of screws you use depends on what kind of wall you have. If you're working with a hollow, wood-frame wall, the easiest and safest approach is to drive support screws through the plaster or drywall, and

DRILLING TIPS

Compared to the old-style brace and auger bit, making holes with an electric drill is easy. Here are a few good drilling tips, so your holes will be round, straight, and properly angled.

■ Drill bits often stray from the marked spots, making it hard to start a hole. To keep the bit from sliding, create a small dimple with a center punch before drilling. (A *center punch* can be any kind of tool with a point on one end and a flat surface to hammer on the other.)

■ If you plan to drill large-diameter holes, first make a smaller hole, and then enlarge it incrementally to its final size.

■ Clamp down the wood or metal to be drilled, or place a *backing board*, a protective scrap-wood piece, under the surface. (Using a backing board also helps to make clean holes on both sides of the surface you're drilling.)

■ To drill a perpendicular hole without the luxury of a drill press, line up the shank of the bit with the edge of a framing square, or use a drill with a built-in spirit level.

then into a wall-framing element, such as a stud, header, or plate. Always make sure at least half the screw's length extends into the framing element.

If mounting your shelf to a hollow part of the wall where there's no framing element to screw into, you'll need to first drill holes in the wall and insert anchors or toggles to firmly hold the screws in place. On solid masonry walls, the screws you use to hang your shelves need to work in conjunction with an anchor that expands and grips inside the wall.

Hollow-Wall Hardware Options

Plastic anchors are small sleeves inserted into a drilled hole. Once penetrated by a screw, they expand. Plastic anchors are best used for hanging light-weight and medium-weight shelves. They aren't as heavy-duty as toggle bolts or spreading anchors, but they are removable.

Spreading anchors consist of a bolt and a metal sleeve. The sleeve is inserted through a drilled hole and tapped into the wall. When the bolt is tightened, the sleeve expands against the back side of the wall. The bolt is then removed, slipped through a bracket or shelf, and retightened into the metal sleeve.

Toggle bolts are spring-loaded with expanding wing-like toggles. To use one, drill a hole large enough to accept the compressed toggles, and feed the bolt through

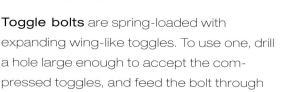

SIX WAYS TO FIND A STUD

For optimum security and strength, always attempt to use studs to support wall-hung objects in your home, such as shelves, artwork, and even towel bars. Studs form the backbone of your home. They're the vertical system of wood or metal framing hidden behind finished walls.

There are many ways to locate the studs behind your walls. Although no single approach is 100-percent guaranteed, if you apply one or more of the following techniques, you can locate studs without too much trouble. Once you find one stud, locating others is fairly easy. Studs, measured from center to center, are usually spaced 16 or 24 inches (40.6 or 61 cm) apart.

■ Use an electronic stud finder. This is a quick and reliable method that works on all types of walls. An electric stud finder detects changes in density. Just pass it over your wall, and a light, display, or tone lets you know when it's over a stud.

■ Use a magnetic stud finder. This easy-to-use tool locates the fasteners that attach drywall to studs. Slide the stud finder over the wall, and its magnetized bar will point to screws, nails, or metallic studs. (Unfortunately, it also points to everything else metal that lies behind your wall, such as pipes, cable, and nails and screws that may be far from studs.)

■ Inspect your baseboards and crown moldings for nails or nail holes, which indicate the presence of studs. Also, outlet boxes for light switches or receptacles are usually mounted to one side of a stud.

■ Shine a light along a wall at a flat angle and look for depressions and seams. Slight dimples can indicate the position where nails or screws fasten drywall to studs. Long vertical seams can show where drywall panel edges meet on a stud.

■ Rap along the wall with your knuckles or with a hammerhead wrapped in a soft towel. This is a popular, though somewhat unreliable, method. If you listen closely, you may be able to distinguish a slightly higher sound over studs and a hollow sound elsewhere.

■ Insert a bent wire clothes hanger into the wall after drilling a hole and missing a stud. Spin the wire to the left and right behind the wall until it hits a stud.

the bracket or shelf to be mounted. Slide the toggles through the drilled hole. They will open on the wall's back side and pull closer to meet it as you tighten the bolt.

Expanding anchors are used on masonry walls. They consist of a lead, plastic, or fiber sleeve with a hollow center to accept a bolt or screw. To use an expanding anchor, drill a hole in your wall slightly longer than and the same diameter as the sleeve. Tap the sleeve into the wall. Slip the bolt or screw through the bracket or shelf you wish to attach, and drive it into the sleeve.

Picture Hangers

The typical picture hanger is a flat piece of sturdy steel bent at both ends with two nail holes in the top. The bend in the bottom end, approximately 45 degrees, forms a hook on which the picture's hanging wire rests. There are two bends at the top end. The first is 90 degrees and the second an additional 45 degrees, bringing the top end of the hanger back to meet the flat metal. Picture hangers are manufactured in different sizes to support different weights. The weight capacity for standard hangers increases in 10-pound (4.5 kg) increments from 10 to 50 pounds (4.5 to 22.7 kg). Several finish options are offered for steel picture hangers, such as zinc plate, brass plate, and white. The accompanying nails are finished to match.

To install a picture hanger, first place it against a flat wall. Next, insert a nail (usually provided) through both holes and tap it with a hammer until a solid connection is achieved. We recommend always using two picture hangers for extra security and to keep your shelves level. If using a picture hanger on a plaster wall, there's a simple method to prevent the plaster from chipping. Prior to installation, simply apply two pieces of cellophane tape in the form of an X at the point where the nail will enter the wall.

Professional Picture Hangers

Professional picture hangers are used by art museums and galleries all over the world. They're available at large home improvement centers. Unique design features make them more dependable, but also more costly. Professional picture hangers are bent only at the bottom end. Their top end is flared with holes that hold one, two, or three high-quality nails. Professional picture hangers won't damage your walls and are easier to install than common hangers. A center-of-gravity channel guides the nails directly into the wall at the perfect angle for a secure hold and allows for no play in the nail. Depending upon the model, professional picture hangers safely hold from 10 to 100 pounds (4.5 to 45.4 kg).

Left: Utility brackets are an important part of this sophisticated shelf design.

Other Picture Hanger Options

Concrete and brick picture hangers are useful when installing shelves on poured concrete, brick, and cinder block walls. Each hanger uses nails manufactured with a spe-

cial finishing tip that easily penetrates hard surfaces and won't bend when hammered.

Tremor control picture hangers are manufactured with a security clip to prevent objects from falling off walls. Devised for earthquake protection, these clips stop items from falling when bumped, deter theft, and are excellent for use in homes with children.

If you wish to hang a shelf in an area where a stud is not available, you can buy picture hangers in a set conveniently prepackaged with a corresponding screw and a wall anchor or plug. This option takes the guesswork out of matching up these three distinct elements.

Quick Hooks

A one-step quick hook looks like a nail skirted by an angled disk. Small and easily hidden, this simple hook is ideal for hanging shelves with hardware placed high on their back side. To use this hook, place its pointed end in the exact position you wish your shelf to hang. Adjust the hook so the face of the disc is parallel to the wall.

Holding the disc firmly between your thumb and index finger, hammer the nail into the wall until the disc is flush. Use two hooks for heavier items or make sure to drive them into a stud. Two hangers will also keep your shelf hung level.

COMMERCIAL SHELVING ELEMENTS

Prefabricated brackets and boards have many uses in today's home. With a bit of creative thinking you can incorporate mass-marketed shelf parts into winning designs.

Shelf Brackets

A bracket is any type of wall-mounted device used to safely support a shelf. It adds strength where a load is placed and is the simplest way to anchor a shelf to a wall. Most of us are familiar with the commercial styles of brackets, braces, and angles. From the utterly unadorned to the highly ornamental, they're sold in a wide variety of sizes, shapes, finishes, and designs. Here are the unique features of some common mass-market brackets you may wish to use in your home. Shelf brackets can also take many different, more creative forms, as we'll demonstrate later in this book.

Right: Utility brackets support a pair of skateboard shelves (see page 58).

INSTALLING A SHELF WITH UTILITY BRACKETS

What You Need

- Shelf board
- 2 or more utility brackets
- Straightedge, such as a metal ruler or square
- Spirit level, also known as a carpenter's level
- Pencil
- Small wood piece, same thickness as shelf board
- Drill
- Screw anchors or toggles (optional)
- Wood screws, if not provided

What You Do

1. Determine where to hang your shelf, keeping in mind that it's always preferable to mount brackets on studs. Align a straightedge with a spirit level in this position. Draw a line across your wall at this height. Make the width of this line the same measurement as the space between your outside brackets.

2. Lay the small wood piece on top of one bracket. Align the top edge of the wood piece with the pencil mark on either end. Use a pencil to mark the positions of the bracket's screw holes onto the wall. Mark the screw holes for the second bracket on the opposite end of the line, and any additional bracket locations in between.

3. If attaching your brackets to studs, drill pilot holes for the screws at all marked points. If using screw anchors or toggles, drill a hole at each marked point, and then insert them into the wall.

4. Hold one bracket in position, and start each screw. Evaluate and adjust the position of the bracket as needed to make it plumb, and then fully tighten the screws. Repeat this step to install the remaining brackets.

5. Lay the shelf on top of the brackets, and adjust its position until the overhang is equal on both ends. Use a pencil to mark the positions of the bracket's screw holes on each end of the shelf.

6. Remove the shelf, and use an awl to make pilot holes at the points marked in step 5. Place the shelf back on the brackets, and line up the screw holes with the pilot holes. Screw through the bracket's holes to attach the shelf.

NOTE: If you wish to attach the brackets to the shelf before mounting them on the wall, make certain that both the shelf's back edge and the back edge of the brackets are flush.

Utility Brackets

Utility brackets, also known as *steel angle brackets*, are L-shaped metal forms. They have screw holes along their edges so they fasten to a wall. Shelves are then laid across them and screwed down. One side of the L, or *leg*, is usually longer than the other. Most utility brackets have a pronounced center ridge. Utility brackets without this feature are referred to as braces. Most brackets are metallic gray, but coated varieties are also available in white, black, or gold-toned finishes. They vary in length and should be purchased according to the size of the shelf you wish to mount. Liberated from their usual workplace locations, utility brackets can contribute a contemporary twist to any home's decor.

Product designers are constantly adapting the utility bracket's form in ways that make it more versatile and more attractive. Upscaling the choice of metals and adding decorative elements, such as scroll work, are the most obvious improvements. Other more subtle changes have revolutionized the appearance of utility brackets. On some models a simple vinyl front piece snaps in place to hide the mounting screws, unifying the bracket's facade. On the work front, some new brackets have a large hook in the front and below the shelf to accommodate a closet pole, and many heavy-duty types are diagonally braced with an additional length of metal for support.

Standards & Brackets

A *standard* is a strong metal U-shaped rod that mounts to a wall, with the ends of the "U" facing the wall. It has many small vertical slots into which special brackets fasten. These brackets have rear hooks that slip into the slots and lock firmly into place, allowing them to securely support shelves. Extending upward at a 90-degree angle, the front end of the bracket has a slight protrusion to help keep the shelf in place. To correspond to the depths of different shelves, these brackets range in length from 4 to 18 inches (10.2 to 45.7 cm). Using the standards and brackets system is one option for creating a shelving unit that's adjustable. To vary the shelf heights to hold smaller or taller items, simply move the position of the brackets on the standards as needed.

The standards and brackets system is surprisingly accommodating. Standards are available in popular precut lengths to fit practically any space you have in mind. You have a choice of several standard and bracket finishes to suit your decorating style. Choose metallic aluminum, black, white, or gold-toned, or even mix and match standard and bracket colors if you desire. (Standards and brackets from different manufacturers may not be interchangeable. Be sure to test fit your elements in the store.) Once the support system is in place, you can use any type of shelf

TIPS FOR CHOOSING & USING BRACKETS

■ A bracket should support at least three-quarters of the shelf's depth. For example, if your shelf is 9 inches (22.9 cm) deep, you should use brackets that are at least 6³/₄ inches (17.1 cm) deep.

■ For the average display, set one bracket every 24–30 inches (60.9–76.2 cm) along the width of the shelf. This measurement is subject to change, depending upon your shelf materials and the items you choose to store or display. For heavier loads, increase the frequency of your brackets by hanging them closer together, but never space brackets farther than 36 inches (91.4 cm) apart.

■ When attaching a utility bracket to the wall, fix the longer side of its L shape to the wall and its shorter side under the shelf. This position offsets the leverage factor. As noted, the shorter side of the bracket should be almost as long as the shelf.

■ It's always preferable to install shelf brackets into wall studs. This method ensures that your screws achieve the strongest hold, thus providing optimum support for heavier shelves and display items. (Refer to page 13 for helpful ways to locate studs.)

■ Using hollow-wall fasteners, such as anchors and toggles, instead of screwing your brackets into studs, is acceptable as long as you're hanging lightweight shelves that will hold lightweight items. Heavy shelves can put such a strain on hollow-wall fasteners that they actually pull out of a wall.

board that fits across the brackets. Just because the base structure looks utilitarian doesn't mean your shelves have to be dull. Consider using unconventional shelf materials, such as jewel-tone laminates or day-glow acrylic sheeting for a refreshing and inspired new look.

Wood Brackets

Most home improvement centers and larger craft supply stores sell unfinished wood shelf brackets. Many of these have designer edges that would take some advanced woodworking tools and skills for you to accomplish on your own. Precut and ready to use, these brackets can make it much easier to create original shelving. Since you won't have to go to the trouble of beveling fancy edges or cutting complex curves, you can spend more time finishing the brackets using any technique you desire and constructing the shelf that goes on top.

Unfinished wood brackets are frequently made of pine, a receptive choice for most paints, stains, and varnishes. All wood brackets mount flush to the wall and are generally easy to install. Some are even sold with all the necessary hardware. Thin wood brackets with simple forms often have a keyhole hanger mounted on their rear edge. More complex bracket designs, such as those with a backing board, are screwed in from the front through countersunk holes. The screw heads are then covered with plugs that match the bracket wood.

Ropes & Chains

You can use ropes and chains to suspend a shelf or a set of shelves from the ceiling or a wall like playground swings. To suspend a shelf, simply drill a hole near each of its corners, and then thread each hole with rope or chain. Tightly knot the rope or clamp the chain under the shelf to make it secure. Use chain accessories, such as washers, nuts, and bolts, as needed to help stabilize the connection. Attach the completed unit to the ceiling or wall with screw eyes and S hooks. When arranging a suspended shelf display, it's best not to use fragile or heavy items as they could tip and fall should the shelf sway.

Shelf Boards

Manufactured shelf boards are cut to specific dimensions to fit commercial brackets. Their thickness, depth, and lengths vary, according to task. The outstanding features of commercial shelf boards include an acknowledged weight-bearing capacity (commonly noted by the manufacturer) and a surface that deters scratches and stains and is warp-resistant. You also have an assortment of veneer surfaces from which to choose, such as synthetic maple, oak, and white melamine.

If this type of board is not what you picture in your home, there are infinite alternatives. Any type of surface will do, as long it is structurally sound, essentially flat, reasonably thick, and sufficiently weight-bearing. Unfinished wood is the most common choice. It's an accessible material easily cut to any dimension and receptive to countless decorative finishes. Although more expensive and less adaptable, glass is another popular choice for its sheer beauty and sophistication. Other natural materials, such as granite, slate, and marble would make exciting choices, as would contemporary synthetics, such as plastic and acrylic. Whatever variety of material you choose, always make sure to select brackets that fully support the shelf's weight as well as the weight of the objects you plan to display.

Storage Units & Organizers

At first glance, prefabricated storage units and organizers may not appear to have much design potential, but just the opposite is true. Shoe racks need not remain in the closet. Let them make a handsome grid shelf on your wall. Wire shelves no longer need to support dishes in the dark. Free them from kitchen cabinets to make a shiny new plant shelf. Once you ignore their intended purposes, commercial shelves and organizers become ripe for experimentation. They are inexpensive, widely available, and easy-to-assemble (if assembly is needed). Depending upon how they are finished, or where you place them in your home, they can become very impressive design elements.

TROUBLESHOOTING: FALLING & SAGGING SHELVES

Shelves can fall or sag for several reasons. The main culprits for shelves falling are: using the wrong type or size of bracket, installing shelves with screws that are too short, or using hanging hardware unsuited for a particular type of wall. Three primary factors lead a shelf to sag: either the brackets are positioned too far apart; the shelving material is not thick enough to carry the load; or a combination of both conditions exists. The horizontal distance, or *span*, between brackets is an important consideration. Experts base suggested span on three variables: the type of shelf material, the width of the shelf, and the size of the load it must carry. If you have any concerns that your shelves will not safely bear your intended load, please check with a qualified lumber consultant or contractor before purchasing materials for any project.

10 TIPS FOR ARRANGING ATTRACTIVE SHELF DISPLAYS

As if creating a new shelf wasn't entertaining enough, once it's hung there's the additional delight of designing its display. An artful arrangement shows off both your meaningful objects and your personal style. Better yet, you can alter it easily and at will. Although no rules are set in stone, here are some bits of conventional wisdom and popular practices for decorating shelves.

1. Decide what items you wish to display. Eliminate objects that you no longer care for or wish to feature in another part of your home.

2. Spend thoughtful time evaluating the characteristics of the chosen objects. Are they short or tall, rough or smooth, light or dark?

3. Plan to keep within reach the items you use most. This is most important if your arrangement includes both functional and purely decorative objects.

4. Make an initial composition on top of the shelf, and then step back for perspective. (Remember to place heavier and taller objects at the rear of the shelf for safety.) What kind of visual weight does each object bring to the display? Does one side appear too "heavy," while the other is too "light"?

5. Look at the space left between objects. How does this area affect the design? Leave plenty of "breathing space" on your shelves in order to view and appreciate items individually.

6. Shift, add, or remove objects to bring balance and harmony to the shelf arrangement. Eventually, you'll arrive at a pleasing presentation, even with very diverse objects. Subtle adjustments can make a big difference.

7. Step back again and again as each change is made and look at your arrangement with a fresh eye. Can each object be seen? Is the arrangement too sparse or too crowded? Does the composition have a pleasing visual rhythm?

8. Consider arranging small clusters of items (odd numbers work well) or grouping objects with a similar theme. Often you can make a more impressive statement with fewer well-selected and well-placed items. If the grouped elements are all the same size, try varying their heights with small pedestals.

9. Create formality with evenly spaced items if you wish. Placing the tallest objects in the shelf's center and working down in height produces a roughly symmetrical and more austere arrangement.

10. Evaluate the space that surrounds your shelf. Readjust nearby furniture, houseplants, or artwork to complement the new look of your shelf. Hang an additional light or redirect an existing fixture as needed to illuminate your display.

WHAT IS MELAMINE?

Melamine **is a chemical compound, consisting of carbon, nitrogen, and hydrogen. It enables the creation of the hard, glossy surfaces used in decorative surface laminates and in adhesives for the production of water-resistant wood-based panels. Durable and long-wearing, melamine surfaces are also hygienic, non-allergic, and highly heat- and chemical-resistant. White shelf boards are one popular example of commercial melamine use.**

Hardware Accents for Commercial Shelves

A few simple touches can not only spice up the appearance of commercial shelves, but make them more serviceable as well. Whether you wish to get organized, get mobile, or just get stylish, these simple accessories help tailor a shelf to suit your needs.

Cup Hooks

Similar to screw eyes, a cup hook has a steel shaft with one end threaded and pointed like a screw. The opposite end, however, isn't fashioned into a closed ring. It remains open in a gentle C-shaped curve. Cup hooks are traditionally used as kitchen storage for handled mugs, but since they come in many interesting sizes and colors, we think they can be put to more creative use. Attach one or a dozen cup hooks to the edge of or underneath a shelf as key-ring holders, jewelry organizers, or to hang art or office supplies. Some cup hooks even come with a safety latch that fastens across their opening.

Cabinet Handles

A cabinet-hardware renaissance is well underway. Manufacturers are producing more attractive knobs and pulls than ever before. Long cabinet door handles make particularly handsome shelf accents. Mounted horizontally on a side shelf panel, they become small-scale hanging bars for all sorts of items (see the Get Mobile variation of The Easily Altered Cube on page 127). Metal cabinet hardware is available in copper, chrome, brass, nickel, bronze, and iron. You can opt for a brushed, polished, or high-gloss finish. Glass, ceramic, plastic, and wood varieties help fill out the offerings. Most cabinet hardware is sold with a proper fastener, making it an extremely easy add-on element.

Casters

Casters are the tires of the hardware world. They mount on the base of both large and small objects to make them mobile. Depending on their function, casters come in many shapes and sizes and are manufactured from a variety of materials, such as rubber, plastic, and metal. Some are wheel-shaped, while others are spherical; some turn a full 360 degrees, while others only roll in a single plane. Stem casters have a vertical stalk that inserts into a hollow leg, while plate and ball casters are topped with a flat surface with holes for screw mounting. Add a set of casters to the base of a cube or bookshelf, and get rolling!

PROTECTING SHELVES & DISPLAY OBJECTS

There are numerous products that help protect the objects in your home. Whether you're seeking a buffering shield, a makeshift shim, a skid deterrent, or a shock absorber, there's a bumper, pad, or gripper perfect for the task.

BUMPERS

Clear rubber bumpers help prevent movement on hard surfaces. They're often applied at the corners of picture frames to keep artworks hanging straight. This can also be a beneficial practice for shelves. Placing bumpers on the back sides of shelves not only keeps them straight, but also helps to shim the shelf to a level position if it hasn't been hung with flush mounts. Rubber bumpers also make great shock absorbers and scratch protectors for shelf boards, especially glass. Simply peel a self-adhesive bumper off its backing paper and firmly press it into place.

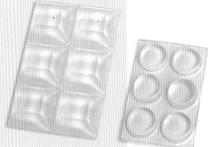

PROTECTIVE PADS

Protective pads are self-adhesive pieces of felt or cork that safeguard tabletops. Just peel one off its backing paper, and apply it as needed to any clean and dry surface. Place protective pads on the base of an object prior to displaying it on a shelf to minimize surface scratches. This precaution is especially rewarding on glass and painted shelves.

GRIPPERS

Grippers protect hard surfaces by acting as a non-skid surface and cushion. Often used under chair and table legs, they marry the soft flexibility of a protective pad with the thickness and skid-guarding ability of a rubber bumper.

ONE-OF-A-KIND
SHELVES & BRACKETS

Opportunities to create fun and functional shelves present themselves in the most unusual places. The projects in this chapter come from hardware centers, toy stores, kitchen outlets, and everywhere in between. Most were discovered by spending time with an attractive object and viewing it from every angle. Sure, the clerks gawked when we turned a trio of letter sorters onto their sides. Other shoppers stared as we held up boxes, baskets, and trays, envisioning them mounted on walls in intriguing configurations. Although this peculiar quest may have raised some eyebrows, it certainly generated some appealing shelf and bracket designs. We hope they inspire you to seek out truly original shelves in unexpected places and make them part of your home.

PAINT BUCKET SHELVES

Galvanized buckets are just as practical and attractive sideways as they are in their normal upright position. No complex metal skills are needed to construct this multipurpose unit. Simply bolt the buckets together, hang them up, and fill them with towels, magazines, or whatever you wish to store.

What You Need

- 3 large metal paint buckets with handles
- 2 small metal paint buckets with handles
- Drill and metal drill bit
- 7 bolts, $1/2$ inch (1.3 cm)
- 7 hex nuts to fit bolts
- Hammer and nail
- Wall screws

What You Do

1. Arrange the buckets in the layout you desire.

2. At the points where the bucket sides meet, drill through both metal surfaces.

3. Run the bolts through the drilled holes, and then screw on the hex nuts.

4. From the back side of the unit, use the hammer and nail to make a hole in the center of the two top buckets. Drive a screw through each of these holes to attach the shelf to the wall.

SHELF CONTAINED

Most consumers merely contemplate what can go *inside* a storage box. How about looking at what can go *on top* as well? Stylish storage boxes are a practical and an attractive solution for containing clutter. A must-have accessory for the well-organized home, the humble box form receives much more attention from today's housewares designers. These items are simply too fashionable to banish to a closet or under a bed.

TOP-SHELF DESIGN

Large, medium, and small drawers can be a great advantage when you're organizing your storage. Different-sized items go in different-sized drawers—perhaps stamps, tape, and clips in the small; scissors, pens, and markers in the medium; and checkbooks and mail in the large. Though quite necessary to own, these types of items are less than pretty to look at, so stash them in a closed drawer.

SAILING BASKET SHELF SET

Y ou can fashion a fantastic shelf from almost any type of basket. These two red beauties are unusually low and wide. Fastened to the wall at two points, each can safely store or display a variety of items, such as a lovely orchid plant.

What You Do

1. Drill two holes on the rim of each basket where the band overlaps. Space the holes as far apart as possible to provide a strong brace.

2. Determine where you wish to hang the baskets on the wall.

3. Attach the baskets directly to the wall using a drill or a screwdriver and screws. Mount them on a stud for safety, or use screw anchors for hollow-wall support.

SOURCING

Baskets are popular and easily obtainable. Traditionally, they're made from natural materials, such as split oak, reed, twig, bamboo, wicker, and rattan. Now you can also find exciting varieties constructed of plastic, wire, or metal mesh. You'll encounter a wide assortment of baskets wherever they're sold, because they're so well-liked and affordable. Whether you prefer a rustic look or one that's sleek and modern, there's a bounty of baskets from which to choose. This incredible selection gives you the opportunity to find the perfect baskets for a new shelf set.

TOP-SHELF DESIGN

Hang as many baskets as you wish in any configuration you can imagine. They'll look spectacular both in a straight line and in a staggered informal arrangement. You could even use different sizes and shapes of baskets in the same display to create a fanciful shelf installation.

STACKED BENCHES & STOOLS

Astacked collection of rustic benches and stools makes an appealing set of shelves. Mellowed with age, their painted wood surfaces make a serene addition to your home decor. Because the individual elements simply rest on top of each other, you can rearrange and add to the collection whenever you wish.

SOURCING

Scouting for benches and stools to stack is a satisfying pursuit for secondhand shoppers. Besides being uniquely beautiful, these items are quite plentiful and reasonably priced. You can fashion an attractive arrangement from an eclectic selection of forms, so pick up any stool or bench that catches your eye.

Before You Begin

Before they're ready to be shelves, some of the benches and stools may need to receive a little tender loving care. To ensure the safety of your display, tighten loose connections as needed with carpenter's glue and finishing nails. Some of the older benches and stools may be a bit wobbly, but there are several ways to make them level. One option is to gently sand the bottom of the longer legs. If you don't want to remove any wood, you can shim shorter legs or attach self-adhesive cork or foam pads.

Shelf Help

• Depending upon their size, your group of stacked benches and stools can sit on the floor or on top of a long bench or table.

• Always place the longest and widest bench or stool at the base of the design.

• Stack pieces in descending order of size, finishing with the smallest bench or stool on top. This pyramid-like structure results in the most stable arrangement.

SECONDHAND DECORATING

Searching for and salvaging objects to use in your home decor is an inspiring adventure. It's a fun way to develop your eye for design and strengthen your shopping skills. Here are some helpful hints for making your hunt for timeworn treasures a pleasant experience.

BEFORE YOU GO

■ **Wear comfortable shoes and casual clothes.**

■ **Dress in layers so you can adjust your attire for changes in weather.**

■ **Carry a bag that will allow you to freely handle merchandise, such as a backpack, fanny pack, or a handbag with a strap long enough to cross over your shoulder.**

■ **Wear a hat or sunblock on sunny days.**

■ **Bring your own shopping bag.**

■ **Pack a tape measure, notebook, and pen.**

■ **Be prepared to pay for your purchases with cash.**

■ **Bring space measurements with you.**

MARKET TIPS

■ **Arrive early for the best selection and the genuine bargains.**

■ **Determine meeting times and places in case you're separated from shopping partners.**

■ **Poke around the displays, looking behind, inside, and under other merchandise.**

■ **Drink plenty of liquids.**

■ **Remember to think of unexpected ways to use intriguing items as shelves—secondhand objects have more character!**

RECYCLED CRATE SHELVES

Instead of discarding wooden boxes and crates, recycle them into shelving units. Their lighthearted and casual appearance will add a touch of comfort to any room. Looking for just the right box is an entertaining hobby. As you make your way from gourmet food shops to flea markets, you might find yourself on a continual scavenger hunt.

10 GREAT CRATES

- Wine bottle boxes & crates
- Fruit & vegetable crates
- Beauty product boxes
- Cigar boxes
- Gourmet food boxes
- Game & toy boxes
- Sports supply boxes
- Jewelry boxes
- Dishware crates
- Art shipping crates

CUSTOMIZE YOUR CRATES

- Stack as many as you like, remembering you can always add more.
- Vary the width, height, depth, and orientation of the crates for visual contrast.
- Trim the boxes with fabric or upholstery finishings, ribbons, or artificial flowers.
- Embellish the boxes with a coat of boldly colored paint or stain. Paint different colors on different boxes if you wish.
- Gild the surface of the boxes with metallic leaf.
- Stencil or stamp the boxes.
- Decoupage the boxes with a collage of images, wallpaper, or color photocopies.
- Carve the box surfaces to create texture.
- Make the boxes a three-dimensional scrapbook.
- Attach mug hooks, towel bars, or other functional accessories.

DRINK CRATE SHELF

Although its glass soda bottles are gone, this vintage drink crate still carries plenty of sentimental charm. Peeling paint and fading logos give the crate a distinctive style. Hung on the wall, it becomes an endearing shadow box shelf with many compartments for displaying small objects.

What You Do

1. Decide if you want to hang your crate vertically or horizontally.

2. Attach two ring hangers to the crate's back side, each approximately 2 inches (5 cm) in from the side edges and 1 inch (2.5 cm) down from the top. (Adjust these measurements as needed to suit the structure and condition of your crate.)

3. At the level you wish to hang your crate, hammer two angled nails or picture frame hangers into your wall, spacing them to correspond to the rings on the crate's back side.

4. Install the crate on the wall, and fill it as desired. Displaying multiples *en masse* creates an effective impression, or you could leave a few of the cubbyholes empty to give the eye a refreshing break.

TOP-SHELF DESIGN

Depending upon how its shelves are dressed, a drink crate can suit many settings. Its most obvious appeal would be to antique enthusiasts with a passion for product design and packaging or for mid-twentieth century collectibles. For a more contemporary look, how about filling the shelves with an assortment of seashells and stones, miniature model cars, dried flowers, or tiny picture frames? On the strictly functional side, a drink crate shelf can be a handy place to organize and store jewelry, make-up, or socks.

STEPLADDER SHELVES

I f you come across an old stepladder, don't throw it away. Even if it's rickety and features many coats of peeling paint, you can stabilize it and create an attractive shelving unit. Generally about 25 inches (63.5 cm) high, stepladder shelves make an engaging display both on the ground and on top of a table.

With its clean lines and attractive blue color, the stepladder pictured above is just the right size to tuck neatly into a corner space. The rungs of the ladder provide convenient space for organizing almost anything. Here, spools of wrapping supplies are neatly kept in check. The height of the stepladder allows the ribbons and cords to hang without becoming tangled.

Some new stepladders are styled like fine furniture. The dark wood model pictured above adds a warm touch to a chilly white bathroom. Much of the bathroom items you use on a daily basis are left out in plain view. Instead of scattering toiletries hodgepodge on precious little counter space, why not arrange containers on top of ladder rungs in a more appealing display? This solution is also immensely practical—you'll find it a time-saver every time you dress.

CANDLE SCONCE BRACKETS

As the popularity of candles has grown, so have the options for displaying them. Sconce-type holders liberate candles from being strictly tabletop ornaments. For the innovative and resourceful decorator, they also make fantastic brackets for wall-hung shelves.

What You Do

1. Determine the distance you wish to leave between the sconces. This measurement is also dependent on the length of your shelf.

2. Mark two level points on your wall at this distance and at the height you wish to hang your brackets. Remember that the maximum distance you should ever leave between brackets is 36 inches (.9 m).

3. Use a pair of nails or screws and a hammer or drill to hang the sconce brackets on the wall.

4. Top your new brackets with a coordinating shelf. Wood, glass, marble, or metal shelves are just a few of your many options.

TOP-SHELF DESIGN

Sconce candleholders come in many enchanting designs. They're made from diverse materials, such as metal wire, wrought iron, and stained glass, and their shapes vary from the very traditional to the very trendy. The calming circular structure and interior spiral design of these particular sconces resembles a peaceful mandala. These uncommon characteristics help to disguise the sconces' original intent, thus making them well-suited for a fluent transition into shelf brackets.

SOURCING

If there are candle stakes fastened to the center of the sconces' bases, their height may interfere with the shelf sitting properly. To prevent this from happening, either carefully remove the top of the stakes with a metal file, or select sconces with deep rims or with no stakes at all. Otherwise, sconce candleholders require no structural modification to make them wall-friendly.

MAIL SORTER SHELVES

The clean lines, even spaces, and warm wood tones of these shelves have an immediate visual appeal reminiscent of both Danish design and the American Arts and Crafts style. Hang several on the wall in an interesting configuration, fill their niches with small-scale objects and collectibles, and few will guess that your remarkable new shelves were once ordinary mail sorters.

Shelf Help

The method you use to hang your mail sorters depends on the type of sorter you choose. For wooden sorters with a thick base, you can attach a single ring hanger. From the back side and near the top edge, screw the hanger onto the sorter. This permits you to mount the shelves flush to the wall on screws. You could also use a keyhole fastener or sawtooth hanger.

TOP-SHELF DESIGN

The vertical dividers on mail sorters usually increase in height from front to back. Here are three ways to use this characteristic to make a wonderful composition.

■ Rotate the mail sorters to determine which way you prefer them to face. The largest surface can be the top or the bottom shelf.

■ Vary the heights at which the individual mail sorters are hung. This breaks up the horizontal lines, altering the look of the installation.

■ Align different shelves on different mail sorters, hanging the units diagonally, or creating a line of shelves that dips or rises in the middle.

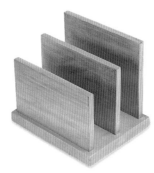

SOURCING

You'll find a variety of contemporary mail sorters at office supply stores and larger home furnishing retailers. They're usually inexpensive, so purchasing multiples will not break your budget. Grouping together three or more mail sorters gives you the most flexibility when you're making your arrangement. Repeating the form more than twice also produces the greatest visual impact.

PLANT STAND SUPPORTS

Multilevel plant stands make unique supports for a set of decorative shelves. Simply select an appealing pair and bridge them with sturdy boards of any material.

What You Do

1. Measure the depth of each plant stand tier to determine the depth of your shelf board. Some depths may vary from level to level. Ours, for instance, is 9 inches (22.9 cm) deep across the top level, and 8 inches (20.3 cm) deep across the bottom.

2. Spread the plant stands apart to see how wide a shelving unit you want to make. Measure this distance from outside edge to outside edge to determine the shelf board's minimum length.

3. Choose what type of shelf board to use. Purchase the boards to fit these measurements, buying one board for each plant stand tier.

SOURCING

You can use new or vintage plant stands for this project. Look for matching pairs at home decor stores, gardening and home improvement centers, and secondhand shops. To ensure level-sitting shelves, make sure all the plant stand tiers are at equal heights.

THRESHOLD SHELVES
& DOORSTOP SUPPORTS

Doorstops make impeccable shelf supports for thin strips of cool white marble. When it's time for tea, you can use them to elegantly display your best demitasse cups, saucers, and spoons. These small shelves express your high style without saying a word.

What You Need

- Marble threshold, 36 x 4 inches (91.4 x 10.2 cm)
- 8 brass doorstops
- Heavy-duty glue

What You Do

1. Take the marble threshold to a ceramic tile cutter, or check with your home improvement center to see if they provide tile-cutting services. Have the marble cut in half so you have two 18 x 4-inch (45.7 x 10.2 cm) pieces.

2. On the bottom side of both marble pieces, measure and mark a straight line 1 inch (2.5 cm) in from both ends. Measure and mark a point 1 inch (2.5 cm) in from each edge on the previously marked end lines.

3. Remove the screws from the ends of the doorstops.

4. Following the manufacturer's instructions, use the glue to adhere the doorstops to the bottom side of the marble pieces, one at each marked point. Let the glue completely dry.

PLANTER BOX SHELVES

Contemporary containers are anything but bland, especially when reconceived as a set of sensational shelves. All you have to do is turn a box on its side to see its potential. Originally designed as planters with a warm, rusted-metal finish, these two shelves are just the right touch for a handsome family room or den.

What You Do

1. For each box, mark at least two points on the base to indicate the position of the wall support hardware. (We suggest a location that's at least 1/2 inch [1.3 cm] down from the top of the box, and 1/2 inch [1.3 cm] inside its edges.)

2. Drill holes through the box's base at the marked points.

3. Place the box on the wall in the desired position.

4. Use wood screws to attach the box to the wall through the drilled holes. For added strength, fasten the shelf into a wall stud or use an anchor for your screws.

5. Repeat this process to install as many box shelves as you wish.

SOURCING

If you're wild about wood, mad for metal, or even have a passion for plastics, you can easily locate boxes to suit your decorating style. We found these examples in a gardening center. A rusted patina disguises the fact that the planters are actually new. On the same shop aisle were shiny aluminum planters, opaque plastic planters, and some made from rough slotted wood. Each variety would make an equally attractive shelf. Also look at secondhand stores, flea markets, and garage sales for inexpensive boxes with abundant character. You can discover plenty of quirky or old-fashioned options.

TOP-SHELF DESIGN

The re-envisioned box-as-shelf is extremely versatile. Hang rectangular boxes horizontally for a wide display, or vertically for a tall one. Cluster multiple boxes together in a very formal or an entirely spontaneous way. Mix and match box shapes and sizes to create an original and eye-catching wall hanging. Place objects inside the boxes as well as on their top surfaces to double your display space.

ONE OF A KIND

WATERING CAN BRACKETS

A cheerful pair of painted watering cans are the perfect brackets for this garden-themed shelf. Topped off with a piece of wood painted in coordinating tones, this shelf will boost your spirits whatever the season.

What You Do

1. Purchase a wooden craft board for the shelf. Its width can slightly exceed the depth of the watering cans. (Our board is 1/2 x 5 1/2 x 24 inches [1.3 x 14 x 60.9 cm]. Our watering cans are 7 1/2 inches [19 cm] high, 14 inches [35.6 cm] wide, and 4 inches [10.2 cm] deep.)

2. Sand the edges of the board so they're smooth, and then wipe off all dust on the board with a soft cloth.

3. Paint the board a color that complements the watering cans. For added interest, you could paint the edge of the shelf board a coordinating color.

4. Determine the back sides of the the watering cans. Mark two level points on the back side of each watering can, each approximately 1/2 inch (1.3 cm) down from the mouth of the can and 1/2 inch (1.3 cm) inside each corner.

5. Use an auger or an awl to pierce the back side of both watering cans at the marked points. Set the watering cans aside.

6. Determine the height for the shelf, and plan how much space you wish to leave between the two watering can brackets. Use a pencil to lightly mark these distances on the wall, making sure your marked points are level.

7. Fasten each watering can to the wall with wood screws threaded through the pierced holes.

8. Set the painted shelf on top of the watering cans, and adjust it from side to side until you're pleased with its position.

SOURCING

Purchase embellished watering cans at home decor centers, or, if you're feeling more inspired, buy plain metal watering cans at craft supply stores and add your own personal touch with acrylic craft paint. Whichever path you take, just make sure each watering can's spout is lower than the top edge of its mouth. (The shelf board will need to sit flat on the mouths of the cans.)

BOTTLE RACK SHELF

It pays to be a smart shopper with an eye for salvage style. This metal bottle rack takes on new life as a bathroom shelving unit. After a touch of restoration, it becomes a pretty and practical storage space for towels. Fold them flat or roll them up to create a charming display.

Shelf Help

Unless you prefer the aged look of recycled metal, you'll want to clean and perhaps finish or paint the shelves prior to introducing them into a room.

Here are a few suggestions for making salvaged metal shelves shine.

Cleaning

• Use a soft cloth or sponge and wash the shelves with a mild detergent, such as hand-dishwashing liquid, and lukewarm water.

• Wipe the metal clean with pure water.

• Dry it with a cloth or paper towels to avoid water spots.

Prepping

• Knock off any rust flakes with a wire brush.

• Clean the surface of the shelves with something more abrasive, such as a scouring powder made with pumice, synthetic scouring pads (not steel wool), or mild solvents, such as denatured alcohol. This process creates *tooth*, meaning the metal is slightly rough, making it more receptive to finishes.

Painting

• Prime any rusty areas with a metal primer paint. This step provides added protection by preparing the surface for a smoother finish coat, improving the adhesion of the top coat, and preventing surface rusting. Follow the directions and drying times indicated on the primer paint can.

• Use an acrylic latex brush-on paint or an oil-based spray paint to color the metal.

Sealing

• Apply a coat of clear acrylic spray or spray lacquer, or rub on a thin coating of paste furniture wax, beeswax, or paraffin. Use these methods on both painted and non-painted metal.

Caring

• Periodically dust your reconditioned shelves with a dry or slightly dampened cloth, or a vacuum cleaner brush.

• Touch up even small chips or scratches to prevent rust.

SOURCING

When salvaging a metal object to transform into a shelf, think about how much weight it may have to support. A very rusty or brittle piece may be too shaky to serve your needs. You want a piece of furniture to last, so look for one that's structurally sound even if it needs a bit of reconditioning.

THINGAMAJIG SHELF

Keeping your eyes and mind open is the best way to discover alternative shelving for your home decor. This blond wood shelf came from the kitchen department of a large housewares store. We think it's a dish drainer, but don't ask us to swear under oath. The important thing is that we saw it on the aisle and knew right away it could be a super shelf.

TOP-SHELF DESIGN

Because it's made from unfinished wood, you could embellish this shelf in many different ways. Along with decorative finishes, three-dimensional ornaments, such as tacks, tiles, or trim, would make a nice addition.

BRACKET FASHION

The style of visible brackets deserves as much attention as the shelf that sits atop them. The Thingamajig Shelf and its brackets are so alike it seems they were made for each other, but, in actuality, the combination was a happy accident. The softly curving L-shaped brackets were manufactured with two countersunk holes on both interior edges. This feature made it simple to attach the bracket to the wall and the shelf to the bracket with screws. If your display items aren't too heavy, you can mount the bracket above the shelf as shown for a dramatically different look.

TOOLBOX SHELF

An old-fashioned carpenter's toolbox makes a magnificent shelf for the kitchen. Store freshly laundered folded linens inside the box, and hang the dish towel you're currently using on its sturdy dowel. Stack pretty dishware on top to increase your storage.

What You Do

1. Look at the base of the toolbox to determine the best hanging hardware. Near the top edge of the box, install two sturdy hangers spaced apart for maximum support.

2. Determine where you want to hang your toolbox shelf. Mark two level points on the wall at this height. Space them to accomodate the hanging hardware attached to the toolbox.

3. Fasten two screws into the wall at the points marked in step 2. Hang the hardware over the screws.

SOURCING

This particular toolbox is a refinished antique purchased secondhand from a stall market. Because its design is a classic, this type of toolbox is still being manufactured today. It's a popular choice for storing craft materials and gardening tools, so you'll be able to locate a new one with ease.

TOP-SHELF DESIGN

Although loaded with nostalgic charm, this toolbox shelf is surprisingly adaptable to many contemporary kitchens. Even in the sleekest of settings, its pale wood and clean lines make it a timeless and refreshing accent piece. Feel free, however, to change the color of yours with paint or stain if you wish. You could also add screw hooks below or to the sides of the shelf to store such items as mugs or pot holders.

DRAWER SHELVES

Look closely at these unique bedside shelves, and you'll see that they're actually two wall-mounted drawers. The one on the left is installed upside-down so its base becomes a surface for the lamp, vase, and frame. The right drawer faces up, creating a compartment for storing books. The drawer runners give the design extra originality.

What You Do

1. Finish your drawer shelves to your liking.

2. Determine where to hang them on the wall. Set them flush or space them apart if you wish. Keep them level or stagger their heights.

3. Attach the shelves directly to the wall using a drill or a screwdriver and screws. If possible, mount them on a stud for safety, or use screw anchors for hollow-wall support.

S O U R C I N G

Surplus drawers are easy to find, and you can use as many as you like to construct a set of shelves. Perhaps you already have a chest you're ready to throw away. Why not recycle its drawers? With some simple sanding and embellishment, such as a fresh coat of paint, a stencil, or stain, they'll take on an entirely new look. You can also find inexpensive drawers at yard sales, flea markets, and thrift stores. They don't have to be fancy to become fanciful shelves.

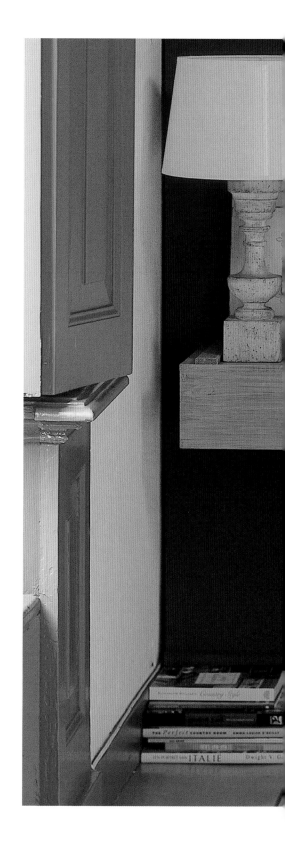

SHOWER TOTE SHELVES

For a lively and practical set of shelves, why not line up rows of sideways shower totes? Today's plastics are so stylish, you can easily integrate them into your decor while creating plenty of inexpensive storage.

What You Do

1. Measure the distance between two of the shower tote's bottom drainage holes.

2. Use a pencil to mark two level points on the wall the same distance apart.

3. Partially fasten a screw into the wall at each of the marked points.

4. Slide the tote's drainage holes over the screws. Check the position of the shelf, and then fully tighten the screws.

5. Repeat this process to hang as many shelves as you desire. Maintain an equal gap between the shelves, or stagger their placement for a playful look.

TOP-SHELF DESIGN

This versatile shelf system can grow and change with your needs. Hang as few or as many plastic baskets on your wall as you wish, knowing you can add more later. Use an assortment of colors or hang a monochromatic installation. Stack your shelves vertically, line them up horizontally, or arrange a multilayered grid. The fresh new shapes and luscious colors of mass-market plastics are irresistible!

WIRE VESSEL SHELVES

Create an easygoing style by mounting two metal containers on the wall. Whatever you choose to display will show through the lightweight metal wire. These wide-mouth vessels can hold all types of things, so you can change their appearance whenever the spirit moves you.

RED WAGON SHELF

The little red wagon continues to be an icon of childhood. It's a simple toy that inspires young minds to take fantastic voyages, nurturing their imaginations. It's easy to prolong this exciting journey. Just hang a red wagon shelf in your child's room, and let the magic linger.

What You Do

1. Purchase a miniature version of the classic metal wagon. These smaller versions have all the same features as their full-size counterparts, such as working wheels and swiveling handles.

2. Determine one side of the wagon to be the front of the shelf.

3. Mark two points on the flat back side of the wagon. Each point should be 1/2 inch

(1.3 cm) under the wagon's rim, and 1 inch (2.5 cm) inside its left and right curves.

4. Use a drill with a metal bit to make a hole at each of these marked points.

5. Determine where you want to hang the wagon on the wall, and mark a level line at the top edge of the wagon.

6. Place the screws through the drilled holes and fasten them to the wall.

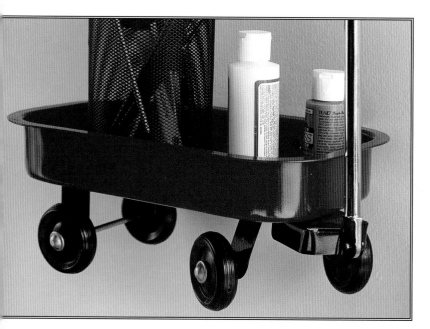

TOP-SHELF DESIGN

With its raised edges, the wagon is a great place to store your child's toys. Fill it with art supplies, blocks or balls, or let stuffed animals take their own wild and enchanted ride.

ULTIMATE AIR SKATEBOARD SHELVES

Both you and your child will find these sports-themed shelves totally extreme. Designed for wear and tear on the street (with a human on board, no less!) these decks can carry any heavy load. Mix and match bright plastics for an outrageously bold look, or use traditional wood skateboards as shown for a chilled-out style.

What You Do

1. Use a ruler or tape to measure the maximum depths of the boards.

2. Take these figures with you to your local home improvement center or hardware store. Select inexpensive metal utility brackets, two for each skateboard, that correctly fit the depth of the skateboards. If the brackets are not sold with hardware, make sure to pick up some screws while you're shopping.

3. Determine where to place the brackets on the bottom of the skateboards, separating the brackets to provide maximum support. (Typically, 1 to 2 inches [2.5 to 5 cm] inside each wheel is a good position.) Make sure to align the back side of the brackets with the back edge of the skateboard so the shelf hangs flush.

4. Use a drill and screws to attach the brackets to the skateboards.

5. Play with the spacing and heights of the boards to create a pleasing arrangement; then fasten the shelves to the wall.

TRAY & PLATTER SHELVES

Convert a tray or platter into a shelf, and the result will be truly original. With limitless styles from which to choose, you're sure to find just the right one to enhance your home design. Sturdy brackets can support almost any type of shelf you can imagine, from a lightweight lacquer item to a weighty ceramic piece.

What You Do

For the Gold Tray

1. Determine how far apart you want to hang the brackets. Mark these locations on the wall with a pencil. (These brackets were manufactured with a set of keyhole fasteners near their top edge.)

2. Calculate and mark the precise spacing for the screws needed to support the brackets.

3. Fasten the screws into the wall. Slide the brackets' keyhole hangers onto the nails.

4. Position your tray. Permanently secure the tray to the brackets. (We inserted a screw through the surface of the tray and into the top of the bracket.)

For the Ceramic Tray

To demonstrate how easy it is to interchange shelf elements and create an altogether different look, we used the very same set of shelf brackets to support the ceramic tray,

but with one very clever twist. Instead of hanging the brackets on the wall in the expected direction, we rotated them, turning the longer flat surface up to brace the shelf.

1. Change the orientation of your brackets. (In this formation, the original keyhole fasteners can not be used.). Drill one hole near the top edge on each side of both brackets.

2. Determine how far apart you wish the brackets to be hung. Mark these locations on the wall with a pencil, making sure the marks are level.

3. Hold the bracket on the mark, insert a screw through the drilled hole, and attach the bracket to the wall. Repeat this step for each hole on both brackets.

4. Position the tray on top of the brackets. Because of their extended length, the brackets safely hold the ceramic tray. If you wish to further stabilize it, you could attach self-adhesive rubber bumpers to the bottom of the tray. These bumpers provide extra gripping strength.

CHAIR SHELVES

Small-scale chairs serve many purposes—some are created for children's seating, some are intended for play, while others are purely decorative objects. Whatever their original function may be, one thing is certain: they all make magnificent shelves.

What You Do

1. Drive two screws into the wall at a slight angle for each chair (a single screw will work for very small chairs). Leave enough of the screws exposed to support the uppermost chair rail. This length will vary according to the chair you're hanging.

2. Hang the chair rail over the screws. Adjust the heights of the screws as needed so the chair's seat (your shelf) is level.

3. Place any object you wish to display on the seat of the chair.

4. Anytime you need to reclaim your shelf to use as chair, just lift it off the screws.

THE INCREDIBLE SHRINKING CHAIR

SMALL

- Children's chairs are emphasized in this installation. Most are scaled down versions of adult chairs, but you can also include high chairs for variety.

SMALLER

- Many lovely little chairs serve as doll furniture. These much-adored accessories, often used for impromptu tea parties and theatrical productions, take many shapes and are made from many different materials.

SMALLEST

- Tiny dollhouse miniatures won't hold a lot when hung on your wall as shelves, but consider including a few in the mix. (Sit a dollhouse chair on top of another chair shelf for a bit of witty decorating.)

SOURCING

You can find secondhand children's chairs at many weekend sales. Take a leisurely trip around your neighborhood on a beautiful spring day, and follow the yard signs wherever they may lead. You're more than likely to come across delightful children's chairs at reasonable prices (and you might make a new friend or two!). If you're really lucky you may find a handcrafted chair or one painted with a folk art or an ethnic motif, but keep in mind that you can paint, stain, or finish any chair to coordinate with your decor. If you don't find the chair of your dreams or your leisure time is limited, head over to larger flea markets and antique malls. The prices might be a bit higher at these venues, but they'll probably have a wider selection of chairs.

SALVAGED POT RACK SHELF

Pot racks aren't just for holding pots and pans anymore. When you find a great one, new or old, hang it within easy reach instead of high above your head. This way, you'll be able to store all sorts of things on its shelves, hooks, rods, and rungs.

SOURCING

As with all antique shelves, make certain to select a pot rack that is structurally sound. Loose parts or severely rusted metal will not be a reliable foundation on which to place objects. Once you find the perfect (or nearly perfect) pot rack, take it home; clean it up; and paint, polish, or seal it to your liking. (Refer to page 46 for tips on restoring and refinishing metal. One soapy bath and coat of clear acrylic spray can make a surprising difference!)

TOP-SHELF DESIGN

By stacking elements above a workstation, you can create a multi-level shelving unit with lots of room for storage. This kitchen installation features a painted wood shelf hanging above the metal pot rack. Wire baskets and other metal accessories coordinate with the pot rack's style. Other homespun elements contribute to the shelf's overall appeal.

PICTURE FRAME SHADOW BOX

Antique picture frames have the type of character only time can create. These grand, heavily decorated frames are considerably deeper than contemporary styles. So much so that it's quite easy to fashion them into a shadow box shelf of rare beauty for the bedroom, or any room in your home.

What You Do

1. Select a picture frame.

2. Turn the frame over and measure the top, bottom, and side edges adjacent to its opening.

3. Decide the depth of the shelf you want to create. This can equal or surpass the frame's depth.

4. Purchase your lumber based on the collected measurements. (We used 1 x 4 stock.)

5. Following the rectangle shelf instructions on page 140, construct a simple box to fit the back side of the frame and mount flush with its opening.

6. Paint or finish the box as desired. (Ours has a coat of white paint.)

7. Attach the box to the frame with a layer of carpenter's glue, and clamp the pieces together. Toe in small nails at an angle to securely hold the box in place.

8. Attach the picture frame shadow box shelf to the wall with a pair of ring hangers or picture hangers, and enjoy!

SOURCING

Finding the right frame can lead you to some very interesting places. From a relative's attic to an estate auction to a weekend flea market, there are many opportunities to evaluate and perhaps purchase antique frames. By doing so, you will also be recycling and repurposing, taking an item conceived for one purpose and using it in an entirely different way.

ONE OF A KIND

COAL GRATE BRACKET

This decorative, cast-iron coal grate serves as the base for an elegant shelf that would look fabulous in any room. Some heat registers would also work nicely for this project. The more decorative the grate, the better.

What You Need

- Cedar plank or suitable board
- Coal grate or heat register
- 2 spring clamps
- 2 L brackets
- Colored pencil
- Drill with assorted bits
- 2 round-head bolts with nuts
- 2 washers
- Wrench
- 2 wood screws, size depends on depth of the shelf material
- 2 small flat ring hangers
- Screwdriver

What You Do

1. Position the board on top of the grate so the back of the board is flush with the back of the grate.

2. Clamp the board and grate together.

3. Find the best location for the L brackets, keeping in mind that the brackets will hold the shelf together. Mark the placement of the screw holes in the brackets with the pencil.

4. Once the bracket holes are marked, remove the clamps from the shelf, and clamp the grate to the work surface.

5. Drill the two marked holes where the bracket will be bolted to the grate.

6. Attach the brackets with the bolts using the washers and nuts.

7. Reposition the board, making sure the pencil marks on the bottom of the board correspond with the bracket holes.

8. Screw the board to the brackets.

9. Along the back of the shelf, attach the flat ring hangers.

10. If your grate is heavy, hang the shelf from two studs if possible, or use suitable hollow-wall anchors.

SUSPENSION SHELF

Unless a shelf breaks with tradition, it's likely to go unnoticed. The easiest way to garner attention is with an unusual shape or color, but eye-catching designs can also come from inventive shelf supports. Rope loops brace this shelf, making it a more dynamic structure.

Shelf Help

The rope loops will not magically hang in the air, so you'll have to devise a way to suspend them from the wall or ceiling. There are many attractive hooks that can do this with style.

• Use easy-to-install screw hooks or screw eyes for interior or exterior shelves. No screws and bolts are required. Simply twist the sharply pointed threaded ends into the wall.

• If you wish to hang your shelf from the ceiling, consider using swag hooks. These are frequently used to hang planters, wind chimes, lamp chains, and curtain sashes.

• Depending upon the thickness of the rope, the weight of the shelf, and the aesthetic you wish to achieve, a wardrobe or utility hook may be a fitting option.

SOURCING

Stroll down the hardware aisle at your local home improvement center, and you'll see an amazing variety of ropes and cords for sale. From the thinnest twine to the sturdiest woven cable there's a cord for every project. Synthetic ropes come in many colors, so you're no longer limited to natural hemp tones. Sturdy through all-weather, synthetic ropes could suspend an exterior shelf on your deck or patio. Always buy more rope than you think you'll need—you'll want to have plenty of length with which to experiment. Once you select it, you can play with ways to weave or braid the rope's ends. You may also want to tie a knot in the loop under the shelf for support.

PEG BRACKETS

Mount pegs on white blocks and neatly install them in a row for a dramatic shelf. There's sufficient space between the base and end of the pegs to hold framed artwork. Place a stained and varnished board across several pegs to create a display surface for smaller objects.

What You Need

- Wood board for blocks, the width of your choice (ours is 1 x 6)*
- Measuring tape
- Pencil
- Handsaw*
- Sandpaper*
- Paint, color of your choice
- Paintbrush
- Deep hanging pegs with mounting screws, as many as you wish
- Drill
- Pliers (optional)
- Shelf board to fit within pegs (ours is a 36-inch [.9 m] piece of 1 x 6)**
- Wood stain, paint, and/or varnish of your choice

*If you use commercial pre-cut and pre-sanded wood blocks, these supplies will not be necessary. You may also skip step 1.

**This shelf board should span the number of pegs you desire with sufficient overlap to securely carry the weight of any objects you display.

What You Do

1. Determine the measurements for the backing blocks. Mark the board to this size, and then use the handsaw to cut as many blocks as you wish. Sand the cut edges of the backing blocks. Wipe off any dust or debris with a paper towel or cloth.

2. Determine the peg location on the block and record the measurements for this point. (Our pegs are centered left to right but are slightly closer to the bottom edge for visual interest.)

3. Paint the side edges and one surface of each block, and let dry. Mark the peg location measured in step 2 onto each of the painted blocks.

4. Mark the points on the wall where you wish to install the block-mounted pegs, making sure all points are level and equidistant.

5. Using a bit slightly smaller than the peg's mounting screw, drill a pilot hole through each block at the marked points. Use the same bit to drill pilot holes at each point marked on the wall in step 4.

6. Insert one peg's mounting screw into the drilled hole of one block, and turn. Once the screw is through the block, position its tip in one of the pilot holes on the wall. Turn the peg tightly to secure, using a pair of cloth-wrapped pliers if necessary. Repeat this step as many times as needed to complete the installation.

7. Finish the shelf board as desired and lay it across the pegs.

CORNER SHUTTER SHELF

Put some old bead board and a matching pair of shutters to wonderful use in this uncomplicated, yet quite satisfying, shelf.

What You Need

- Piece of cove molding
- 2 matching shutters, 4 to 6 feet (1.2 to 1.8 m) high
- Tape measure
- Handsaw
- Framing square
- Finishing nails
- Hammer
- 1 x 2 board, for shelf supports
- Scraps of bead board or tongue-and-groove flooring

What You Do

1. Cut the cove molding to the height of the shutters.

2. Form a 90-degree angle with the shutters, and insert the cove molding into the space created behind the shutters.

3. Check the angle of the shutters with the framing square, and nail the cove molding to each of the shutter frames.

4. Measure the inside dimensions of the attached shutters to determine the dimensions of the shelf supports.

5. Cut the 1 x 2 stock to make the shelf supports. Each support will need two pieces that form a 90-degree angle.

6. Nail the supports together, using the framing square to check the angles.

7. Cut and nail pieces of bead board or flooring diagonally to each shelf support. Use the framing square to check the angle of the cuts. The finished shelves should fit flush inside the shutters.

8. Space the shelves equally apart, and nail them to the shutter frames.

9. Cut two pieces of bead board or flooring to the height of the shelf for the shelf trim.

10. Nail the bead board or flooring to both sides of the unit.

11. Cut and nail pieces of bead board or flooring diagonally to the top of the shutters. Create a 1-inch (2.5 cm) overhang if desired.

ONE OF A KIND

CINDER BLOCK ALTERNATIVES

The cinder block system is a perennial dorm room favorite. It's an efficient method of stacking boards spaced by masonry blocks, bricks, milk crates, or any other cheap yet sturdy item. Although this is a highly effective way to make shelves in a hurry, the end result is aesthetically numbing at best. Here are some artful alternatives.

Before You Begin

Always stack the foundation elements for your shelves in a straight, even column. This helps prevent your shelves and the objects they support from falling. (Although we're wholeheartedly in favor of asymmetry in design, we can't, in this instance, overlook the unwavering principles of gravity and the laws of physics.)

SILVER PILLARS

These sparkling columns, intended to hold pillar candles, make fantastic supports for a set of glass shelves. Their classically refined contour is a graceful addition to any room.

Many ordinary pillar holders have a pointed stake fastened to the center of their base. The bottom of the candles are driven onto this stake for protection. If its point rises above the rim, this stake interferes with the shelves sitting properly on the pillars. To prevent this from happening, either carefully remove the top of the stake with a metal file, or select pillars with deep rims and no stake. Purchasing deeply rimmed pillars with a recessed candle base leads to another decorative option. You can cleverly fill the recessed space with ornamental materials, such as colored sand, dried flowers, and seed beads.

GLASS VASES

Turned upside-down, multiple flower vases make a sparkling set of sophisticated shelf supports. Purchase inexpensive but sturdy glass vases with wide mouths. You'll find many designs from which to choose at discount home decor stores. Our vases are tall and square in shape with an elevated block grid. Their stability produces a firm foundation while their relief pattern casts light and shadow in fascinating ways. To create level and flush shelves, make sure to select vases of equal heights that sit flat. Use bumpers or protective pads to buffer the points where the shelves touch the vases if you wish. Install this exceedingly radiant and incredibly useful shelf set anywhere you want to reflect a luminous style.

TEA TINS

Metal tins are often printed with intriguing designs. Find a pattern that appeals to you and purchase several tins to support an enchanting set of shelves.

Tea tins are frequently rectangular, making them an excellent shape for foundation

blocks. Different flavors of tea may be packaged in identical containers that vary in printed design. In this installation, the color of the tin alludes to its contents: raspberry, lemon, peach, green—and Earl Grey!

Tea tin lids are often slick. In order for your glass shelves to establish a firm grip, you may want to attach self-adhesive rubber picture frame bumpers. Simply peel them off their backing paper, and firmly press one in each corner of each tea tin lid. (Because the bumpers are clear, they won't interfere with the smart style of your shelves.)

DECORATING
SHELF SURFACES

An unfinished shelf is like a blank canvas waiting for an artful touch. In this section, we took six conventional prefabricated shelves and handed them to talented designers. Each one was decorated in a different way, using techniques such as painting, upholstering, and tiling, to show you the incredible adaptability of a simple shelf. The results range from a traditional shelf with elegant layers of molding to a totally cosmic shelf with stars and moons. One of these shelf projects is sure to inspire you to create your own custom-made masterpiece.

CEILING TILE SHELF

Textured wallpaper replicates the look of antique embossed ceiling tiles. Its surface is primed for painting and receptive to many decorative flourishes. Here, it covers an unfinished shelf and is studded with copper tacks.

What You Need

- Unfinished wood shelf
- Textured wallpaper
- Scissors
- Decoupage medium
- Foam brush
- Spray paint, flat black
- Spray paint, copper
- Rub-on wax, gold
- Polyurethane spray, satin finish
- Copper tacks
- Small hammer

What You Do

1. Determine the placement of the textured wallpaper on the shelf, making it straight and level to look like copper ceiling tiles.

2. Wrap the wallpaper around the shelf as you would wrap a gift. Start the paper on the back side of the shelf. Roll it out and over the front edge to the bottom of the shelf, trimming it around the shelf's brackets. Leave enough paper overlapping the shelf's side edges to wrap around to the bottom.

3. Cut pieces of the textured wallpaper to fit both sides of each bracket. Cut out additional pieces to fit the front edge of both brackets.

4. Once you're sure of the fit, apply the decoupage medium to the top surface of the shelf. Position the custom-cut wallpaper, and smooth it into place. Apply more decoupage medium to the edges and bottom of the shelf, and smooth down the cut paper, wrapping the side edges over like gift wrap. Apply decoupage medium to the brackets, and attach the cut wallpaper. Let the paper dry on the shelf.

5. Following the manufacturer's instructions, spray the whole wallpaper-covered shelf with the flat black paint. Let dry.

6. Spray the shelf unevenly with the copper paint, leaving much of the black paint exposed. Use your fingers to lightly apply the gold wax over the embossing, covering only the raised portions. Let the paint and wax dry.

7. Following the manufacturer's instructions, spray the whole shelf with two thin and even coats of the polyurethane. Let the sealant completely dry.

8. Decide where on the textured paper "tiles" to attach the copper tacks. Lightly hammer them into place.

DECORATING SHELF SURFACES

UPHOLSTERED SHELF

Contemporary synthetic suede fabrics come in all the colors of the rainbow. This particular shade of sky blue makes a lovely upholstered shelf. It's easy to accomplish this star-studded look: simply make a paper pattern, cut out and adhere the fabric, and embellish it with tacks.

What You Need

- Unfinished wood shelf
- Large paper for pattern making
- Scissors
- Straight pins, pencil, or erasable pen
- Synthetic suede fabric, 1/2 yard (45.7 cm)
- Craft glue to use on fabric and wood
- Foam brush
- Upholstery tacks or nailhead tacks
- Small hammer

What You Do

1. To make a paper pattern, start at the top edge of the back side of the shelf. Wrap the paper around the front shelf edge, and then onto the bottom of the shelf. Cut the paper to fit around the brackets.

2. Cut the pattern so the outer two edges of the paper will meet in the middle of the shelf board's top edge. (The seam of these two edges will later be covered with upholstery tacks.)

3. Create a pattern for the brackets, with the edges of the paper meeting in the middle of the front edges of the brackets.

4. Place the pattern on the back side of the synthetic suede material. Pin it in place or trace its outline with a pencil or an erasable pen. Cut out the fabric, remove any pins, and then make certain that the pattern parts fit the shelf.

5. Evenly apply a layer of craft glue to one side of one of the brackets. Carefully position the synthetic suede material onto the bracket. Apply glue to the front edge of the bracket, and then wrap the fabric over the edge. Repeat this step to cover each side of both brackets. Be careful not to get any glue on the top of the synthetic suede.

6. Evenly apply a layer of craft glue to the top surface of the shelf. Carefully position the synthetic suede material on top of the glue. Apply craft glue to the front edge and to the bottom of the shelf. Wrap the fabric around the edge and onto the bottom of the shelf. Carefully smooth down the fabric. If you make a mistake, you can gently adjust the fabric before the glue dries.

7. Use the small hammer to nail in the upholstery tacks. Make an evenly spaced and level line of tacks around the top edge of the shelf and down the edge of both brackets. Working with *nailhead tacks*, those prefabricated in an even row, will make this step much easier to accomplish.

DECORATING SHELF SURFACES

MOCK LEATHER SHELF

Brown paper bags and white craft glue are all you need to achieve this handsome surface treatment. Wad the paper while it's wet to create subtle variations in color and texture reminiscent of softly aged leather. Add a brass curtain rod and finials to the shelf's brackets for an elegant (and useful) finishing touch.

What You Need

- Assorted brown paper bags (different stores have different colors)
- White glue
- Large mixing bowl
- Unfinished wood shelf
- Polyurethane spray, satin finish
- Drill
- Drill bit, 1/2 inch (1.3 cm)
- Brass curtain rod, 24 inches (60.9 cm) long, 1/2-inch (1.3 cm) diameter
- Pipe cutter or hacksaw

What You Do

1. Tear the brown paper bags into various shapes and sizes. Make the pieces any size you want. Keep all the pieces from each bag in a separate pile. (Paper bags from various stores have distinct colors, but, at this stage, it's often hard to tell the difference. Making individual piles now helps you stay organized later.)

2. In large mixing bowl, thoroughly mix equal parts of white glue and water. (We used 1 cup [237 ml] of each.)

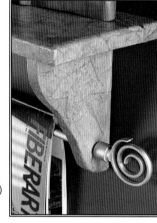

3. Dunk a piece of the torn paper bag into the glue mixture. Pull it out, and then wrinkle it, squish it, and wad it up. (This gives the paper texture and color.) Open up the piece of wadded paper, place it anywhere on the shelf you desire, and flatten it down.

4. Repeat step 3 to cover the whole shelf, making sure to alternate between different piles of paper. You can overlap the pieces and tuck them around the shelf corners. You can even stop working on the project and come back later, as long as you cover up the glue mixture. Once the shelf is fully covered with paper bag pieces, let it completely dry.

5. Following the manufacturer's instructions, spray at least two coats of the satin polyurethane onto the shelf.

6. Determine where on the brackets you want to place the brass rod, and mark these points, making sure they're level. Drill a hole through each bracket at these marked points.

7. Use the manual pipe cutter or hacksaw to cut the brass rod. The rod must extend past the bracket holes a sufficient distance to accommodate the brass finials. Attach one brass finial to each end of the brass rod.

GLASS TILE MOSAIC SHELF

Easily accessorize a painted wood shelf with rows of mosaic tiles. These colorful squares of glass have an intrinsic and a mesmerizing beauty. Adhere them side-by-side with glue for quick and dazzling results.

What You Need

- Unfinished wood shelf
- Wood putty
- Small putty knife
- Sandpaper
- Primer paint
- Acrylic paint, color of your choice
- Small paintbrush
- Glass tiles
- Tile nipper
- Glue*

Use the glue recommended by the manufacturer of the glass tiles you purchase.

What You Do

1. Following the manufacturer's instructions, use the wood putty to fill any imperfections in the shelf. Once dry, sand the filled areas as well as any other rough edges.

2. Use the primer paint to cover any knots on the shelf surface. More than one coat of primer may be needed. Let it completely dry between coats.

3. Paint the shelf with one or more coats of the acrylic paint. Allow each coat to dry before recoating.

4. Glue the glass tiles to the front edge and to both side edges of the shelf. Use the tile nipper to trim tiles to fit as needed. Glue additional glass tiles along the edge of both shelf brackets. Let the tile glue dry overnight.

DECORATING SHELF SURFACES

DECORATING SURFACES

STARRY, STARRY NIGHT SHELF

Junior astronomers will love the look of this heavenly shelf hanging in their room. Brightly colored moon and star ornaments dance on coiled springs of wire. Easy to assemble, this project can be modified for any color scheme. May it bring a whole galaxy of sweet dreams for your little ones!

What You Need

- Unfinished wood shelf
- Wood putty
- Small putty knife
- Sandpaper
- Primer paint
- Paintbrush
- Assorted acrylic paints (we used opalescent paints)
- Wooden ornaments, assorted star and moon shapes
- Small paint brushes
- Wire brads
- Hammer
- Wood glue
- THNN wire*
- Drill and drill bits
- Wood dowel or broom handle
- Pliers

You can find this colorful plastic-covered electrical wire in home improvement stores.

What You Do

1. Following the manufacturer's instructions, fill any imperfections in the unfinished shelf with the wood filler. Once dry, sand the filled areas as well as all other rough edges.

2. Use the primer paint to cover any knots on the shelf's surface. More than one coat of primer may be needed. Let it completely dry between coats.

3. Paint the shelf with one or more coats of acrylic paint in the color of your choice. Allow each coat to dry before recoating.

4. Use the acrylic paints to decorate the star and moon ornaments as desired. (We added dots of a contrasting color around the edges of each ornament. To do this, lightly dip the end of a small paintbrush handle into acrylic paint, and then gently touch the handle end to the edge of the wood ornament.) Let the paint dry.

5. Use the wire brads to attach some of the painted wood ornaments directly to the shelf edges. Add a drop of wood glue to the back of each ornament before nailing it to the shelf. Sink each wire brad below the surface, and then fill the depression with wood filler. Once dry, sand the filler and touch it up with matching paint.

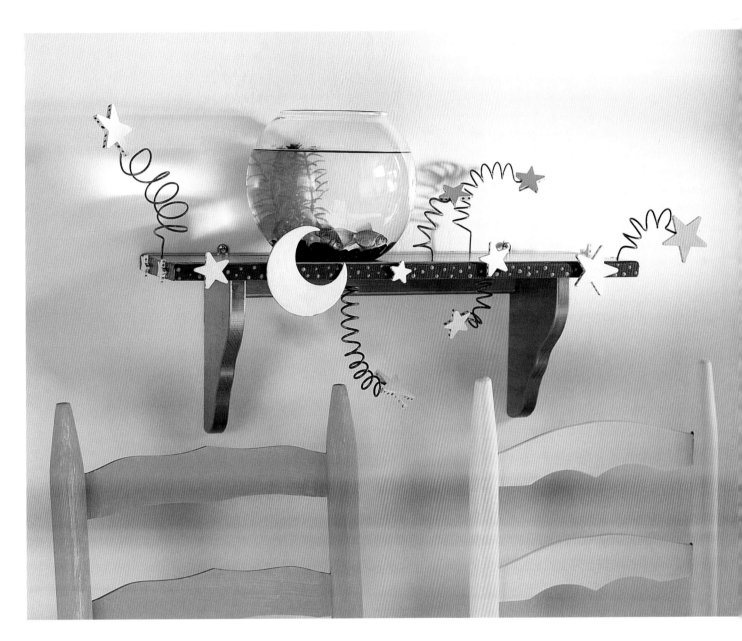

6. Choose a drill bit approximately the same diameter as the THNN wire. Drill one hole in the bottom edge of a painted wood ornament and one corresponding hole on the shelf.

7. Coil a length of the THNN wire six or eight times around the small dowel or broom handle, and then slide it off. Bend each end of the coiled wire with pliers. Slip one end of the wire into the drilled hole in the bottom of the wood ornament. Slip the wire's opposite end into the hole drilled in the shelf. If desired, add a bit of glue to secure the wire in the holes.

8. Repeat steps 6 and 7 as often as you wish to attach additional wire coils and wood ornaments to the shelf.

CLASSICAL SHELF

By simply adding a couple of pieces of decorative molding, you can transform a plain shelf into one that's elegant and refined. There are numerous molding designs from which to choose. Simply pick out an appealing pair at your local home improvement center. This shelf's high-gloss white finish is radiant and versatile, but use any color of paint that flatters your interior decor.

What You Need

- Unfinished wood shelf
- Sandpaper
- Measuring tape
- Dentil molding, 8 feet (2.4 m)
- Handsaw
- Drill and drill bit
- Finishing nails, 3/4 inch (1.9 cm)
- Hammer
- Small braid molding, 8 feet (2.4 m)
- Miter box
- Wood putty
- Small putty knife
- White primer paint
- Paintbrush
- Spray paint, white gloss or color of your choice

What You Do

1. Thoroughly sand all surfaces of the unfinished shelf.

2. Measure the length of the shelf's side edges. Measure and cut two pieces of the dentil molding to that dimension. When measuring the molding, make sure to leave at least half of a dentil piece intact on both ends for strength. Also make sure that each side piece has the same pattern.

3. Position the side pieces of dentil molding on the shelf. Drill small pilot holes through the molding and the shelf at the points where they will join. Nail the side pieces of molding in place with the 3/4-inch (1.9 cm) finishing nails.

4. Measure and cut the front piece of dentil molding for the shelf. It should span the entire front edge of the shelf as well as cover the edges of the side molding pieces. Make sure the dentil patterns are identical at both ends. Drill small pilot holes through the molding and the shelf at the points where they will join. Attach the front piece of molding to the shelf with the $^3/_4$-inch (1.9 cm) finishing nails.

5. Measure the side edges and the front edge of the shelf over the newly installed dentil molding. Measure and cut three pieces of the small braid molding to fit to these dimensions. On both ends of the front piece, use the miter box to cut the molding at a 45-degree angle. Cut a 45-degree angle on one end of each side molding piece, leaving the other ends square.

6. Drill small pilot holes through the small braid molding and the shelf at the points where they will join. Attach the pieces of small braid molding to the shelf with the $^3/_4$-inch (1.9 cm) finishing nails. Gently sand the attached molding.

7. Following the manufacturer's instructions, use the putty knife and wood putty to fill in all nail holes and cracks. Let the putty dry and sand it smooth. Wipe off the shelf with a clean, lint-free cloth.

8. Paint one coat of the white primer onto the shelf, and let dry. Lightly sand, and then clean the shelf. Following the manufacturer's instructions, spray the entire shelf with the spray paint. Apply at least two even coats. If you wish, add more thin coats of paint to produce a shinier, more opaque finish.

SHELVES IN FORGOTTEN SPACES

Slowly examine your living space, room by room, floor to ceiling, and look for unusual places you could hang a shelf. Do you notice any unoccupied areas above doorways, below windows, or along stairs where a shelf could be added? Could you use these vacant spaces to create attractive visual displays or valuable storage surfaces? Acting on this simple exercise could add a lot to your home.

CORNER ACCENT SHELF

Everyone likes surprises, and there are plenty of ways to accomplish this when you decorate your home. Hanging an accent shelf in a secluded location, such as between a door molding and the corner of a room, is an unexpected treat.

Although it's small, this sconce shelf provides a vital focal point in an otherwise vacant hallway. Its pronounced profile extends far from the wall, giving more depth and contour to the boxy room.

Matching the shelf to the molding was the right decision for the color scheme and style of this room. However, if your walls aren't painted so dramatically, you may want to select or create a different shelf. Paint it a vibrant color as a contrast to white walls, or cover it with gold leaf for a more formal appearance. Whatever surface treatment you choose, you'll be adding a surprising and unusual touch to a small, forgotten space.

BENCH & ARMREST SHELVES

This clever bench provides such an abundance of shelving and storage that seating almost becomes its secondary purpose. The two deep shelves directly below the seat are most prominent, but look also at the oversized armrests and see two more shelves at your service!

The space under seats is not so much misused as it is ignored. With the exception of the deacon's bench, a traditional furniture piece designed with a chest as its base, few seats incorporate storage. Here, however, this idea is achieved with considerable flourish. The items chosen for the shelves are pretty enough to be seen yet not entirely essential (or fragile for that matter—swinging heels and wagging tails will do no damage

here!). Surplus throw pillows and magazines are the small indulgences you can take comfort in having nearby. Atop these wide shelves they stay both organized and accessible.

More often than not, armrests are, as their name implies, built for only one purpose. Their width rarely varies. However, this storage bench features armrests with an increased surface area that accommodates much, much more than arms, hands, and elbows. With two supporting brackets, the bench's armrests are constructed just like basic wood shelves. These broad surfaces become additional areas on which you can make artful arrangements.

STAIRWAY SHELVES

Whether they lead to second story bedrooms, a finished basement, or a home office area, stairways are notorious space wasters. With the addition of shelves, an adjoining wall reclaims much of the lost space by making the area more functional and attractive.

This design uses simple cube shelves that are easy to build (see page 138 for step-by-step instructions). The multiple cubes are vertically stacked in pairs and installed in an ascending manner. The top cube of the lowest pair is hung on the same level plain as the bottom cube of the next, middle, set. This arrangement provides an attractive symmetry to the overall look of the shelves.

Keep in mind that you can increase or decrease the depth of the cubes depending upon how much stairway space you have. Even thin shelves with minimal decorations will improve the look of a blank wall.

WINDOWSILL SHELF

Breakfast nooks and other small spaces leave little room for cumbersome furniture. This isn't an obstacle, but rather an opportunity to create unique display shelves and storage units.

A windowsill shelf is the simple extension of the sill itself. To achieve this stylish look (and valuable surface!) just attach a wider board directly to the sill. Purchase a piece of wood that exceeds the width and depth of your windowsill. Draw the shelf shape you wish to create on the board, and cut it out with a saw. Sand the cut edges of the wood smooth.

Attach the extended shelf by countersinking wood screws directly into the sill surface. Carefully fill the hollows with wood putty to disguise the screws, and then finish the shelf as desired. Paint or stain the board to match the walls as shown, or introduce a new highlight color or faux effect.

You can create a shelf measuring over twice the original sill width if you wish. Simply make sure to reinforce the new surface with brackets or angle irons, one at each end. These supports provide the additional security required for your new shelf to be strong and durable.

NEW LOOKS & USES FOR COMMERCIAL SHELVES

For the resourceful home decorator, even mass-market shelves have plenty of design potential. In this chapter, we make ordinary shelves extraordinary by using them in surprising places, hanging them in unusual configurations, and even giving them a new purpose. You'll see such things as shelves transformed into a child's make-believe kitchen, a simple bracket shelf taking the place of a window box, and a sconce shelf used as part of a framed, three-dimensional still life. Other ideas are small wall variations with a big impact, such as painting a solid block of color or hanging a wallpaper panel behind a row of shelves. Since you won't be making the shelves, you'll have ample time to experiment with their placement, design, and appearance.

BEDSIDE SHELVES

An alarm clock, eyeglasses, reading material, and a good lamp are just a few of the things you might need next to your bed. Although most people use an entire table (or even two!) to hold these items, an attractive set of shelves can be a superb alternative.

THE BENEFITS

• Price

You can purchase a set of well-designed commercial shelves at a fraction of the cost of a table. (Choose unfinished wood, and you'll save even more money.) This might inspire you to use interesting embellishment techniques, such as decorative painting, that you wouldn't dare try on more expensive furniture. Customizing the shelves can also make them integral to the design style of the entire room.

• Style

With so many commercial shelves on the market, you can find a shape to suit any decor. These shelves have a pattern of gentle curves flowing around their edges. This detail sets a fresh and romantic tone in keeping with the room. Dark rich wood shelves with heavy molding would work well in a manor-style bedroom; whereas, a sleek brushed aluminum pair would be the right touch for an urban loft setting.

• Size

Perhaps your bedroom is small, and you need to squeeze the most out of limited space. Eliminating tables and replacing them with bedside shelves causes more of the floor to show, creating a more spacious impression.

• Upkeep

Less floor-dependent furniture also means fewer places for dust bunnies to hide. Cleaning under bedside shelves is definitely easier than maneuvering around tables.

SHELF PORTRAIT

This intriguing shelf composition looks like a painting come to life. A thick picture frame borders a carved sconce shelf. The shelf provides a three-dimensional base for flower arrangements or any other artful object you wish to display.

SOURCING

Here's another secondhand decorating idea for antique enthusiasts and bargain hunters alike. The two treasures you'll be seeking are a large-scale decorative picture frame and a substantial sconce shelf. Look in the usual secondary markets as well as in shops that specialize in architectural salvage until you find just the right pair. (If your goal is to fill a particular wall space in your home, remember to bring along measurements.)

TOP-SHELF DESIGN

Painting the area inside the frame a different color than the rest of your walls would give extra prominence to the floral arrangement or any other object you wish to display.

What You Do

1. Find a sconce shelf and an interesting frame.

2. Leave them in the state in which they were found, or refinish them to suit your style. You could strip and refinish the wood, gild the surfaces with a layer of gold or silver leaf, or apply a coat of paint or stain.

3. Attach two hangers to the back side of the top of the frame in order to install it to the wall. Evenly space the two hangers, each approximately 3 to 4 inches (7.6 to 10.2 cm) in from the frame edges and 1 to 2 inches (2.5 to 5 cm) down from the top. This ensures the installed frame remains level.

4. Hang the frame with hooks or screws.

5. Determine where to position the shelf, making certain to leave plenty of room for a stunning floral display, and securely install it on a stud or with a hollow-wall fastener.

EXTERIOR WINDOW SHELF

Elevate summer's blooms to eye level with an exterior shelf. Conspicuous from inside and out, it's a versatile option for the creative decorator. Taking the place of a traditional window box, this shelf adds more flexibility and visual interest to your home year-round. Throughout the growing season, different plant species flower at different times. With a window shelf, you're free to rotate your pots, and continually display plants at their peak.

INDUSTRIAL CHIC SHELVES

Let sleek-looking wire shelves bring a sophisticated and contemporary style to your home. Although primarily manufactured for commercial use, they quickly and effortlessly conform to modern decor. With an abundance of rewarding features built in, industrial shelving units work wonders in any room.

THE BENEFITS

• Strong

Because of its heavy-duty steel contruction, each shelf can hold from 300 to 500 pounds (136 to 227 kg).

• Flexible

You can assemble utility shelves rapidly without any tools.

You can mount the shelves on feet you can level to your floor or on top of casters to make it mobile.

You can adjust the shelves up or down in 1-inch (2.5 cm) increments along the lengths of its vertical posts.

When your storage needs change, you can transform this highly versatile unit in an instant.

Left: This tall living room unit has a unique warehouse charm. Aluminum shelves are strong enough to support a small collection of books and works of art, but they aren't as muscular as steel.

• Tidy

An open-weave shelf structure significantly reduces dust accumulation and permits a free flow of air.

• Bright

Light penetrates each shelf, giving you greater visibility of stored items. For the same reason, wire shelves are particularly friendly to plants and flower pots, letting them soak up the sun.

Right: Chrome-plated 18-gauge steel makes this three-shelf kitchen unit as sturdy as it is stylish. Sitting on bright metallic surfaces, colorful kitchenware looks especially vivid.

SOURCING

There are many places you can find appealing industrial shelving units. Several adventurous retailers offer their own designs specifically intended for home decor, but there are other, more unconventional outlets for you to consider. Think about the original consumers of industrial shelves, and go directly to their sources. Warehouse, janitorial, educational, and commercial kitchen suppliers are a good bet, as are office furniture markets. Some shops even offer used merchandise from the trade. This is a fantastic opportunity to get a great bargain and to do your part to recycle and reuse. Just remember to bring your measurements with you. Industrial shelving units cannot be cut to size, but they're manufactured in a standard selection of widths, depths, and heights.

A CHILD'S DELIGHT

How low can you hang a shelf? How about low enough for easy child access? Installed near the floor, these prefabricated shelves are in the perfect place for little ones to grab their toys for an afternoon tea party. To the delight of parents, children can also pick up after playtime.

SAFETY TIPS FOR CHILDREN'S SHELVES

■ Always take your child's head clearance into consideration.

■ Hang the bottom shelf about waist high and the top shelf above his or her head, but still within reach.

■ Teach your child that shelves are not for climbing.

■ Store heavier items, such as books and blocks, on the lower shelf, and lighter items up high.

■ Purchasing shelves with softly rounded edges is a good precaution.

TOP-SHELF DESIGN

Use plastic storage boxes on top of the shelves to hold small toys and multi-part games, such as puzzles. This is an inexpensive way to contain the clutter your child is bound to collect, and it helps to maintain a tidier appearance on the shelves. Removing the boxes from the shelves leaves your child with plenty of room on which he or she can draw, play with clay, or pursue other creative activities requiring a flat, sturdy surface.

SHELVES FOR PLAY

There are countless ways to expand your child's creativity. These unique shelf ideas are two of the most clever we've seen. Just the right size for a pretend kitchen and office, they will fuel hours of imaginative play.

Shelf Discovery ▶

In the photo on the right, a budding chef carefully watches over his soup du jour. His pot rests on a small shelf conveniently hung at arm's reach. Four black circles painted on the surface of the shelf simulate stovetop burners. For a child, this simple embellishment is enough to open a whole world of culinary delights.

While his soup simmers, perhaps this child will put the kettle on for an afternoon tea party. Hanging a second ledge above the stove shelf establishes an accessible place for him to neatly store his dishware.

◀ Shelf Taught

On the opposite side of the kitchen wall sits an aspiring artist (see photo, left). Two similar shelves facilitate her passion for expressing her world through pictures. She can pull up a chair to the lower shelf for a level and sturdy desk. The upper ledge provides ample space for art supplies and a framed drawing or two. This arrangement also serves as her personal space for effective after-school study.

SHELF ILLUMINATION

I f you have a favored spot in which you like to read, study, or work at home, creating adequate lighting is essential. Attaching a light below a flat shelf is an easy and attractive alternative to overhead fixtures or tabletop lamps. By using a prefabricated shelf, you can complete this installation in a single afternoon and enjoy your new nightlight (and a good book!) that very evening.

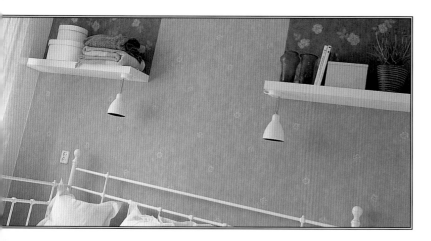

What You Do

1. Select a light fixture that mounts to a ceiling or wall in the design that's right for you. Look at everything from industrial metal task lights to sleek glass sconces to more complex track systems, and you'll find a great under-shelf style.

2. Determine where to mount your shelves. Take the length of the lamp and head clearance into consideration. You won't want a bright light shining directly in your eyes, but you will want it close enough to benefit from the extra illumination. These factors will more often than not lead you to hang your shelves much higher than anticipated.

3. Install your overhead shelves, following the manufacturer's instructions and making sure that they are secure and level.

4. Mount one lighting fixture on the bottom surface of each shelf. The position of the fixture on the shelf is up to you.

SOURCING

There are many light fixtures from which to choose. Permanent fixtures screw into the shelves, and their bases remain in one place. Temporary fixtures generally clip onto the shelf edges, and you can move them from location to location at will. The rod of the fixtures can be rigid, beaming a fixed shaft of light, or flexible (also known as *gooseneck*), letting you aim light wherever you wish.

TOP-SHELF DESIGN

Standard incandescent bulbs are well-equipped for handling under-shelf lighting, or you may want to fit the fixture with a spotlight bulb for additional drama. To brighten the items on top of the shelves, make the best use of natural (outside) light. A window above or next to your shelves will provide illumination as well as a view.

SHELF INDULGENCE

Imagine this bedroom without the horizontal cube shelves. It would appear rather drab; don't you think? Visually exciting and exceedingly functional, these stylish rows of shelves provide ample storage and display opportunities, and it's simple to achieve this look in your own home.

What You Do

1. Determine the height at which to hang the shelves on the wall and decide how much space you want to leave between them. A large and compact grouping creates an intense visual impact. However, you certainly may alter the number and spacing of your shelves to fit your room and to achieve the desired effect. It would be quite dramatic to significantly raise the level of the installation to a point just under ceiling height, to hang the cubes at different levels, or to even stack a few.

2. Use a level and a pencil to lightly mark your wall at the desired height.

3. Following the manufacturer's instructions, hang your cube shelves in the desired positions.

SOURCING

Many retailers stock cube shelves. You can purchase the most basic variety at your local home improvement center. Just look in the storage and organization department. Here you're likely to find white cube shelves manufactured with a synthetic veneer that require some minor assembly. These models are economical, which is a key consideration since you'll be buying them in bulk. If this style is not to your liking, you may have success shopping at home furnishing warehouses. They're more likely to sell a wider variety of designer cubes. If you're inclined to do-it-yourself projects, feel free to construct the cubes from wood, following the easy instructions on page 138.

TOP-SHELF DESIGN

More is more. In this room, the sheer quantity of shelves makes such a strong impression that they require no further embellishment. Their white veneer provides a cool and sedate surface for the materials on display. As storage cubbies, the open cubes hold plenty of decorative and functional accessories, cleverly replacing bedside tables. Inside the closed cubes is an equal amount of space in which to hide personal belongings. The cube tops offer even more room for decorating. Bud vases, framed photographs, and lamps comfortably fit on these surfaces, as do a pair of clip-on task lights.

A COLLECTOR'S MEDLEY

Whether you're a bona fide collector or simply drawn to unique types of objects, chances are good you've gathered decorative items that would make a fabulous wall display. Painting multiple commercial shelves an attractive color, and then hanging them in a formal pyramid creates a distinct focal point you'll really enjoy.

What You Do

1. Determine a height for the bottom row of shelves. Use a carpenter's level to lightly mark a straight line on your wall spanning the width of the entire row.

2. Install the center shelf. Once this element is in place, hang the left and right shelves, spacing each of them one bracket-width away from the edge of the center shelf.

3. Determine how much vertical space you want to leave between rows.

4. Use the level to lightly mark a straight line on the wall that spans the width of the entire middle row.

5. Align the top edge of one shelf with the marked line. Beginning on either the right or the left, center the shelf bracket between one of the gaps on the bottom row.

6. Install the first shelf on the middle row. Follow these instructions to position and hang the second shelf.

7. Mark a level line for the top shelf/row. Make the vertical distance between the top and middle rows equal to that left between the bottom and middle rows.

8. Center the bracket of the top shelf between the gap left on the middle row, and install the shelf. Once your dazzling new pyramid is hung, enjoy arranging your prized possessions into a pleasing composition.

SOURCING

Shop for small display shelves you can buy in bulk. Our installation uses six shelves, but you can increase or decrease this amount, depending on the available space and number of objects you wish to exhibit. (Wouldn't you love to see a floor-to-ceiling pyramid, incorporating dozens of shelves?) If you wish to paint them to match your decor, it's practical to select unfinished wood shelves. They're simple to sand, paint, and seal. Properly finished shelves won't chip or peel, and you can easily clean their surfaces.

TOP-SHELF DESIGN

This unconventional shelf installation is as engaging as it is utilitarian. The soothing color and simple contour of the shelves enhance the glass collection's beauty. The installation's pyramid shape subtly pulls the eye upward, heightening the sense of overall lightness.

WALLPAPER PANEL

An inset of pretty wallpaper behind stacked shelves enlivens any ordinary wall. First, paste up the accent panel, and then install light wood shelves with matching brackets. Creative, coordinated, and clean, this look works well in many rooms.

What You Need

- Butcher paper (optional)
- Masking tape (optional)
- Level
- Yardstick
- Scissors
- Wallpaper sizing*
- Prepasted wallpaper**
- Water tray (for soaking prepasted papers)
- Sponge
- Large tray for water
- Paperhanging brush or smoother

*Ask a specialist at your local wallpaper store to recommend the best sizing (preparation coat) for your paper and walls. The right sizing prepares the walls so you can more easily slide your paper into place. It also works as a bonding agent to ensure the paper adheres well, and makes the paper easier to remove later, if necessary.

**Prepasted wallpaper is the easiest to install and is available in many colors and patterns. If you select a wallpaper that isn't prepasted, you'll need to use a brush to coat it with paste, and hang it following the manufacturer's instructions.

What You Do

1. Determine what size wallpaper accent panel you wish to hang. To get a complete picture of the layout, you might find it helpful to make a false panel with butcher paper and tape it to the wall. (To create one neat and tidy line, we cut the width of our wallpaper panel to match the width of our wood shelves.)

2. Prep your walls. Wash and dry them well. Patch any holes or cracks with wall compound. After the compound is dry, sand the patched areas smooth. Remove the covers on any electrical outlets and light switches that are in the way. Cover electrical outlets with masking tape, and remove any heating grates as needed. Primer is a must only if you're papering over new drywall, but it promotes adhesion on any type of wall. Finally, apply a coat of wallpaper sizing, and let it dry.

3. Using the level, mark the position of the panel on the wall. Cut the wallpaper to size.

4. Loosely roll the wallpaper panel, pattern side in, and immerse it in a tray filled with cold water for approximately 15 seconds. Transfer the panel from the water tray onto a flat surface, pattern side down. As it unrolls, make sure the wallpaper panel is wet on both sides.

5. Without creasing the wallpaper, carefully fold the panel with the pasted sides together. Let the panel rest for two minutes to ensure the paste absorbs enough water.

6. Use a smoothing brush to place the panel in position. Work down the center of the panel, and then out to each side, carefully smoothing all bubbles. Once the paper is adhered, remove any excess paste with a damp sponge. Let the wallpaper dry before installing the shelves.

PHENOMENAL FLOATING SHELVES

Flat or floating shelves have caught on big in the world of home decorating, and for good reason. Free from distracting brackets, floating shelves seem to defy gravity by having no visible means of support. You can install them in many ways to serve many needs.

STRAIGHT STACK

The image on the right shows an installation of six floating shelves. Providing plenty of storage, these shelves easily replace an enclosed cupboard or pantry. They keep kitchen essentials clearly visible and within arm's reach. You can even hang your floating shelves at various height intervals to accommodate specific needs without losing any semblance of order. A level shelf installation with even edges keeps the overall appearance neat and tidy. From silly cereal boxes to heirloom sterling silver, whatever you put on these shelves will have instant visual cohesion.

DO IT YOURSELF!

Constructing a floating shelf from scratch is easier than it may seem.

1. Measure the distance between your wall studs.

2. Mark two centered points on the edge of a shelf board corresponding to the stud distance.

3. Drill holes in the shelf board at these two points with a bit that is the same diameter as a heavy-duty lag screw.

4. Determine the hanging height of the shelf, and levelly mark the wall studs at this point.

5. Drive one lag screw into each marked point on the wall studs.

6. Cut off the heads of the installed lag screws.

7. Slide the drilled shelf board onto the projecting screw ends.

COLOR CONNECTIONS

Painting a portion of a wall prior to installing a set of floating shelves is a simple way to achieve a dramatic decor. Here, a panel of cherry-blossom pink serves as a dazzling backdrop for three rich wood shelves. The colors unite to establish a bold and beguiling focal point.

What You Need

- Prefabricated floating shelves, as many as you wish to hang
- Measuring tape
- Pencil
- Calculator (optional)
- Painter's tape
- Paint
- Paintbrush

What You Do

1. Determine how much space you wish to leave between your purchased shelves. (The gaps can be even or can vary in size, depending upon your display or storage requirements.) Add these measurements together.

2. Measure the thickness of one shelf, and multiply this figure by the number of shelves you'll be installing.

3. Determine the space you wish to leave between the top edge of the top shelf and the ceiling (or the top of your painted rectangle).

4. Determine the space you wish to leave between the bottom edge of the bottom shelf and the painted rectangle.

5. Add together the totals found in steps 1 through 4. This figure is the vertical dimension of the painted background.

6. Measure the width of one floating shelf. (Measure the longest shelf if using shelves of different lengths.)

7. Determine how much farther you wish to extend the painted rectangle past the end of the longest shelf. Double this measurement to account for both ends.

8. Add the totals of step 6 and step 7 together. This figure is the horizontal dimension of the painted background.

9. Carefully measure and mark the rectangle on the wall with a pencil, making sure all lines are level and plumb. Firmly apply one edge of the painter's tape directly on the pencil lines. Paint inside the rectangle up to the edge of the tape. Let the paint completely dry. Apply additional coats as needed.

10. Remove the painter's tape and repaint uneven edges as needed. Install the floating shelves, following the manufacturer's instructions.

MAGAZINE SHELF

With just a few supplies from the plumbing department of your local home improvement center, you can transform common commercial shelves into an impressive magazine and book rack. Install pure white shelves to support the reading material and galvanized steel pipes and pipe fittings as attractive enclosures. Whether you collect back issues, have numerous subscriptions, or simply wish to create a sophisticated library, you'll find this a versatile, simple, and stylish shelf system.

Before You Begin

Different magazines have different heights. Taking this into consideration, you may want to leave more room between the bottom two shelves for oversized publications. Conversely, you could leave less room between shelves for storing retail catalogs, books, and television guides. (It's this type of flexibility that makes creating your own shelving system so appealing.)

What You Do

1. Determine how many shelves you wish to hang, and how much space you wish to leave between them. A magazine's average height is slightly less than 11 inches (27.9 cm). Add to this measurement enough room for you to access your magazines with ease. We suggest an additional 2 to 3 inches (5 to 7.6

cm). This space also helps keep your unit from looking too crowded by providing visual breathing room. At this point, you're looking at a total of 13 to 14 inches (33 to 35.6 cm) between the top of one shelf and the bottom of the next.

2. With these dimensions in mind, follow the manufacturer's instructions to hang your shelves, making certain they are solid and level.

3. For each shelf you hang, purchase one galvanized pipe equal to its length and two galvanized pipes equal to its depth. These pipes form the front and side pieces that contain your magazines. To connect them you'll need two 90-degree elbow fittings per shelf. Select fittings that match the diameter of your pipe. Simply screw together the threaded pipes and fittings, or use set screws to connect unthreaded materials.

4. Buy two flanges per shelf, each the same diameter as the pipe. A *flange* is the type of fitting that holds the pipes on the wall. Determine how much distance to leave between the top edge of each shelf and the pipe enclosure. This measurement is both a practical and aesthetic concern. (Your magazines and books need to be secure, but your unit also needs to look good!) The distance can also change from shelf to shelf, depending upon the size of your publications.

5. At the level you wish to hang your pipe, use wood screws to attach one flange to the wall at each end of the shelf. Tightly join the side pipes to the flanges with threads or set screws. Attach an elbow fitting to the open end of one side pipe, and then to the front pipe. Complete the pipe enclosure by attaching the second elbow fitting to the remaining open pipe ends. Repeat this process for each shelf.

PLUMBING PIPE SHELF UNIT

L ike a child playing with building blocks, you can construct the most imaginative structures with pipe. Install this multilayered shelving unit in the bathroom to store frequently used items.

What You Need

- Allen wrench
- 9 rail supports*
- 3 galvanized pipes, each 4 feet (1.2 m) long, 1-inch (2.5 cm) diameter
- 8 single-socket tees*
- 2 galvanized pipes, each 6 feet (1.8 m) long, 1-inch (2.5 cm) diameter
- 6 extra-heavy flanges*
- 2 90-degree elbow joints*
- 2 galvanized pipes, each 12 inches (30.5 cm) long, 1-inch (2.5 cm) diameter
- Wood screws and screws for your wall
- Wood glue
- Finish nails
- 3 pieces of quarter-round molding, each 3 feet (.9 m) long
- 3 lengths of 1 x 8 board, each 3¹/₂ feet (1.1 m) long (for the shelves)
- Paint and paintbrush
- 18 wood screws
- Screwdriver
- 1 x 8 wood for the storage box**

*Kee Klamp® system fittings are used to make this shelf. They differ from regular galvanized pipe connectors in that they are secured to the pipe with set screws. Fittings should be purchased to fit 1-inch (2.5 cm) diameter pipe.

**Exact measurements for the storage box are not given. Assemble the shelf, and then measure the exact distance from flange to flange. Use this measurement to create a simple box form for the bottom shelf, or purchase a ready-made box.

What You Do

1. Slip three rail supports on each of the 4-foot (1.2 m) lengths of galvanized pipe.

2. Slip four single-socket tees on each of the 6-foot (1.8 m) lengths of galvanized pipe.

3. Attach one extra-heavy flange at the bottom of each of the 6-foot (1.8 m) pipes.

4. Attach a 90-degree elbow joint at the top of each 6-foot (1.8 m) galvanized pipe.

5. Attach the 1-foot (30.5 cm) pipes and the flanges to the 90-degree elbow joints.

6. Level the single-socket tees on the long pipes. Attach the 4-foot (1.2 m) pipe lengths to the single-socket tees.

7. Secure the shelf unit to the wall and floor with the appropriate screws.

8. Use wood glue and finish nails to secure the quarter-round molding strips to the wood shelves. If you have a router, you can create a channel for glass or clear plastic sheeting strips as shown in the photo. Paint the wood shelves as desired.

9. Use wood screws to attach the shelves to the rail supports.

10. Measure the distance between the two flanges. Construct a simple rectangle based on that measurement following the directions on page 140.

11. Paint the storage box as desired, and then secure it between the flanges with screws.

THE EASILY ALTERED CUBE

You can effectively adapt a shelf structure, such as a cube or box, to serve many purposes and conform to many styles. These four examples show the incredible versatility of a simple shape. Follow the instructions on page 138 to construct a basic cube, and then refer to these suggestions for creative customizing ideas.

DIVIDE & CONQUER

A cube shelf with vertical dividers will help you stay organized (see photo, above). Paint the cube with a vibrant base coat if you wish, such as this beautiful and intense shade of watermelon. Further embellish its surface with an attractive stencil in a contrasting color, or create an original freehand design.

What You Do

1. On rigid cardboard or foamboard, carefully draw the shape of slim dividers to fit inside the cube's opening. (You can separate the cube into as many sections as you wish.)

2. Using the straight edge of a metal ruler and a sharp craft knife, cut out the dividers slightly outside the marked line.

3. Enhance the dividers with coordinating decorative paper. (We selected a rose and white toile pattern, and then affixed it to our boards with spray adhesive. You could also use a thin layer of decoupage medium or white craft glue.)

4. Slide the finished dividers into the cube shelf and space them as desired. Tension should securely hold them in place. If your dividers are too tall or stick out too much, gently sand their edges with sandpaper or a sanding block, and reinstall. Repeat as needed until the dividers precisely fit into the cube.

5. Adhere a magnetic strip on one or both sides of the cube, near its top edge. This additional feature lets you post important invitations, messages, and reminders in an attractive and attention-grabbing way.

6. Hang your handy new cube shelf on the wall with two evenly spaced and level keyhole, sawtooth, or ring hangers. Assign a slot for your mail or current catalogs. You can even sort and store office supplies.

GET MOBILE

Wouldn't you just love to wake up to the aroma of a café au lait lovingly wheeled into your room on this very modern, very mobile cart? This crisp and clean looking cube has an outstanding feature: maneuverability! You can roll a caster-mounted cube around your home and place it anywhere you need an extra shelf and small tabletop. Paint the cube a neutral color so it will blend into any room.

What You Do

1. Measure the interior width of the cube, and cut a board to this length. To create a recessed shelf, select a board with a width that's at least 2 inches (5 cm) less than the depth of the cube.

2. Sand the cut edges of the board, and paint it as desired. (It could be interesting to paint the shelf a different color than the cube.)

3. Slide the shelf into place, and nail through the sides of the cube to attach. Use two nails on each side of the shelf.

4. Cover the nail heads with wood putty, and then sand and repaint this area once dry.

5. Add one or two large-scale handles to the cube for steering or storage. This is a great opportunity to use chic cabinet pulls or hand-towel bars.

6. Following the manufacturer's instructions, attach the casters to the bottom side of the cube, and it's ready to roll!

MULTITASK

Adding on a few basic items transforms a humble cube shelf into a hardworking multipurpose unit for your kitchen. Construct or buy a basic cube, and then install a horizontal shelf, following the easy instructions for Get Mobile on page 127, to increase the cube's surface and storage area. The base of the cube, the added shelf, and the cube's top are all available to hold cookbooks, dishware, spices, linens—any kitchen item you wish to store.

Thanks to chalkboard paint, this cube also functions as a message center where notes can be left or lists made.

What You Do

1. Determine where on the side of the cube you want to position the chalkboard. Mask off this area with painter's tape.

2. Following the manufacturer's instructions, apply several coats of chalkboard paint to the side of the cube, and let it dry thoroughly. Remove the painter's tape.

3. Use epoxy to adhere a metal tray at the base of the chalkboard to hold chalk or an eraser. (An attractive business card holder might be just the right size.)

4. Complete your kitchen cube with a set of mug hooks. Decide where you want them to hang, and mark these locations. Position the hooks far enough apart from each another to prevent the mugs from bumping. Our hooks are near the front edge of the cube, but you could move yours farther back, if you wish. Firmly screw the mug hooks into the base of the cube. Make sure that, on your final turn, the hooks point forward. Now your cube is fully functional and ready to work for you!

THE EASILY ALTERED CUBE

STAY IN TOUCH

Let a shelf keep your indispensable items close at hand. You can store lots of things both in and on a bedside cube.

What You Do

1. Purchase a cube shelf or follow the simple instructions for building one on page 138. You may attach a back panel, or leave it off.

2. Paint the cube or finish it as desired to complement your room.

3. Choose a set of four well-designed table legs, and use supplied hardware to connect them to the underside of the cube. This decorative element will elevate your cube to a comfortable height as well as set its stylistic tone.

THE EASILY ALTERED CUBE

BUILDING SIMPLE SHELVES

othing beats the satisfaction of creating a project from scratch. For the willing do-it-yourselfer, we've included several simple shelf projects anyone can accomplish. There are many styles from which to chose, such as a stacked unit of boxes and rectangles, a spiffy planter shelf, a quartet of candle ledges, absolutely divine cube floaters—even a workstation to keep your kitchen tidy. Better still, with a fresh coat of paint or some other choice embellishment, you can easily adapt all of these projects to flatter your home. These basic designs don't require advanced woodworking skills or tools. For beginners to get their bearings, or as a refresher for those with experience, we've included some tips on working with wood. This information will serve you well once you choose to build our uncomplicated yet appealing shelves. So put on your work clothes, sharpen a pencil, and transform a simple board into a custom-made shelf.

SIMPLE WOODWORKING

With the basic woodworking skills outlined here, you can build any of the attractive shelf projects on the following pages. Beginners and skilled craftsmen alike may wish to brush up on these fundamental practices prior to creating a shelf from scratch.

CUTTING WOOD

A piece of wood is either *ripped* (cut along its length) or *crosscut* (cut across its width). Specific saws or saw blades exist for each procedure. Every saw removes an amount of wood from the piece you're cutting equal to the thickness of its blade. This waste is called the saw's *kerf*, and you'll need to account for it whenever you make a cut. The kerf should always be on the waste side of the cutting line.

With a few exceptions, you can make all of the cuts necessary for the shelf projects in this chapter with a common handsaw. Just keep in mind that making correct cuts with a handsaw requires extra time and patience. The most popular power-cutting tool is the circular saw. Its blade adjusts to cut at a 90-degree angle, 45-degree angle, or any angle in between. With a circular saw, you can use a combination blade that rips or crosscuts.

Other Saw Options

A coping saw consists of a steel, U-shaped frame with a very thin blade fastened across its opening. Use a coping saw to make curved and interior cuts on wood less than 2 inches (5 cm) thick. A backsaw is often used to make smooth joinery cuts with the use of a miter box. A jigsaw is a power saw used to cut curves, shapes, and large holes in boards. A router is an advanced handheld power tool that cuts decorative shapes and round edges, creates grooves and notches, and makes joints.

SANDING

You can sand any of these simple shelf projects by hand. Use common sandpapers designed specifically for wood, decreasing the coarseness of the grit as you sand. An inexpensive plastic sanding block or an electric palm sander will smooth wood surfaces faster.

SIMPLE WOOD JOINTS

The projects in this book use either butt joints or mitered joints to attach wood pieces. Butt joints are a simple right-angle connection. The end of one board abuts another, leaving one end grain exposed. A butt joint must be reinforced with fasteners, usually carpenter's glue and nails or screws. Miter joints are formed at an angle, usually 45 degrees, cut perpendicularly across the width of a board. Two mitered boards join together to make a right angle without exposing the end grain of either piece. This provides a finished, all-wood corner appearance. Miter joints must be reinforced with screws or nails (see instructions, right).

FASTENING

Select screws and nails that penetrate the second thickness of wood as much as possible without passing through its opposite surface. Make sure that if you wish to countersink screws you use the flat-head variety. Driving nails at an angle rather than straight in produces a tighter hold. This process is known as *toenailing*. With some practice you can even toenail screws. For exterior shelves, galvanized steel nails and screws provide good weather resistance. Finally, don't be stingy with fasteners. If there's the slightest chance that a joint could be shaky, add a couple of extra screws or nails.

MITERING

Mitering molding and wood for joints is a relatively simple wood cut requiring nothing more than a miter box and a backsaw. Refer back to these instructions whenever a project calls for a mitered joint. (You can also miter corners with a circular saw, a compound miter saw, or a table saw.)

What You Do

1. Place the wood piece you're cutting in the miter box, butting it hard against the box's near side.

2. Place a piece of scrap wood under the wood to be cut so the saw runs through without damaging the bottom of the miter box.

3. Make sure the blade is aligned in the correct slats (45-degree angles in most cases). For best results, measure your project pieces after the first cut. However, if you have already measured the piece to be cut for the project, make sure the saw cuts the angle without altering the measurement.

4. Hold the backsaw in one hand, with the index finger pointing along the blade. With your other hand, firmly hold the wood to be cut. Pull the saw toward you for the first few strokes, and then push it away from you to deepen the cut. Use steady, smooth strokes, letting the weight of the saw do most of the work.

Pilot Holes

Drilling pilot holes for nails and screws prevents wood from splitting. For nails, drill the holes about two-thirds the length of the nail and slightly smaller in diameter. For screws, use successively sized drill bits to first create a pilot hole, which should be about half the diameter of the screw, and then a shank hole, which should be the same diameter as the screw's shank.

WOOD PUTTY, PLUGS & COUNTERSINKS

The easiest way to cover screw and nail holes is to use wood putty, also known as wood filler, a colored plastic substance that hardens when exposed to air. Try to match the filler to the final color of the wood, or use a filler that can be painted or stained.

Predrilling holes for countersunk screws is normally a two-step operation. First, drill a pilot hole, and then a countersunk hole, slightly larger in diameter than the screw head. (If you use the same size screws on a regular basis, you may wish to invest in a combination pilot-countersink bit for your drill, which performs both operations at the same time.)

The countersunk portion of the hole should be just deep enough to allow the screw head to sink below the wood surface, or it can be deep enough to accept both the screw head and a wood plug insert. Wood plugs can be purchased or made by cutting off slices from a wooden dowel. Dip the plug in a small puddle of carpenter's glue, start it into its hole, and tap it into place with a hammer. Allow the glue to dry, and then trim the plug with a chisel.

FLOATING BOX SHELVES

This shelf style is particularly popular in contemporary decorating. Follow the directions below to create your own trio of floating box shelves, and then install them horizontally, as shown, or vertically.

What You Need

- 6 pieces $1/4$-inch (6 mm) plywood, each 12 x 12 inches (30.5 x 30.5 cm)

- 6 pieces $1/2$-inch (1.3 cm) board, each 12 x 3 inches (30.5 x 7.6 cm)

- 6 pieces $1/2$-inch (1.3 cm) board, each 11 x 3 inches (27.9 x 7.6 cm)

- Carpenter's glue

- 2 bar clamps

- Try square

- Finishing nails, 1 inch (2.5 cm)

- Hammer

- Nail set

- Putty knife

- Wood putty

- Sandpaper

- Level

- Wood screws, $2^1/2$ inches (6.4 cm)

- Drill with countersinking bit and screwdriver bit

- Interior-grade enamel paint, in the color of your choice

- Paintbrush

Note: You may paint the boards prior to constructing the box shelves, but the wood-putty-covered nail holes will have to be touched up after installation.

What You Do

1. Place a bead of carpenter's glue on the ends of two of the 11-inch-long (27.9 cm) boards. Butt their ends with two of the 12-inch-long (30.5 cm) boards to form a 12 x 12-inch (30.5 x 30.5 cm) box.

2. Clamp the box together. Check that it's square and adjust as needed.

3. Fasten the edges of the box together with the 1-inch (2.5 cm) finishing nails. Use a hammer and nail set to disguise any nail heads, and then fill the holes with wood putty. Let the putty dry, and then sand.

4. To form the bottom of the box, center and fasten one 12 x 12 x $\frac{1}{4}$-inch (30.5 x 30.5 x .6 cm) plywood piece to the edges of the connected boards with carpenter's glue and finishing nails. Sand all edges flush.

5. Repeat steps 1–4 to construct two more box shelves to this point.

6. Use the level to make a hanging guideline on the wall. Using $2\frac{1}{2}$-inch (6.4 cm) wood screws, fasten the back side of the boxes to the wall at this marked line.

7. Fasten the remaining 12 x 12 x $\frac{1}{4}$-inch (30.5 x 30.5 x .6 cm) boards to the tops of the boxes with carpenter's glue and wood screws. Use a countersinking bit to drill a pilot hole and countersink all screw heads. Fill all remaining holes with wood putty, let dry, and then sand.

8. Mask the wall around the box shelves with painter's tape. Paint the shelves the color of your choice with the interior-grade enamel.

BUILDING SIMPLE SHELVES

CUBE & RECTANGLE SHELVES

Stacked cubes and rectangles make very versatile shelves, providing you with ample and distinct surfaces on which to compose a number of small visual tableaus. Constructing these basic forms is an easy project you can quickly complete. Leave them freestanding, or mount them to a wall if you wish. Try mitering the corners for added refinement.

What You Need

- Tape measure
- Handsaw
- 8 1 x 12 boards, each 12 inches (30.5 cm)
- 8 1 x 12 boards, each 24 inches (60 cm)
- 16 1 x 12 boards, each 10 inches (25.4 cm)
- Carpenter's glue
- 2 bar clamps
- Try square
- Finishing nails, 2 inches (5 cm)
- Hammer
- Nail set (optional)
- Putty knife (optional)
- Wood putty (optional)
- Sandpaper (optional)
- Interior-grade polyurethane (optional)
- Paintbrush (optional)

Before You Begin

Use a tape measure to ensure all cut boards are the correct dimensions and are square.

What You Do

For the Cube Shelf

1. Apply a bead of carpenter's glue to the cut ends of two of the 10-inch-long (25.4 cm) boards. Using two of the 12-inch-long (30.5 cm) boards, assemble a 12-inch (30.5 cm) square cube, with the 10-inch-long (25.4 cm) boards as the inside pieces.

2. Clamp the cube together, and check that it's square. Adjust as needed.

3. Use finishing nails to attach the glued edges. To hide the nail head, hammer only to within $1/8$ inch (3 mm) of flush, and then countersink the head with a hammer and nail set.

4. Use a putty knife to apply wood putty to the nail holes if desired. Allow the putty to dry; then sand.

For the Rectangle Shelf

1. Apply a bead of carpenter's glue to the cut ends of two of the 10-inch-long (25.4 cm) boards.

2. Using two of the 24-inch-long (60.9 cm) boards, assemble a 12 x 24-inch (30.5 x 60.9 cm) rectangle. Use the two glued 10-inch-long (25.4 cm) boards as the inside pieces.

3. Clamp the rectangle together, and check that it's square. Adjust as needed.

4. Use finishing nails to attach the glued edges. To hide the nail head, hammer only to within 1/8 inch (3 mm) of flush, and then countersink the head with a hammer and nail set.

5. Use a putty knife to apply wood putty to the nail holes if desired. Allow the putty to dry; then sand.

For Multiple Shelves

1. Using the remaining lumber, repeat the instructions to build more cube and rectangle shelves, until you complete four of each type.

2. Sand and finish the boxes as desired, and then arrange the shelves against the wall.

Right: This rectangle shelf variation is wall-hung. It features mitered joints.

CANDLE LEDGE QUARTET

It takes only a few supplies and a small amount of time to build these charming accent shelves. Finish the basic wood form in any decorative style, and then hang them on your dining room wall. With each holding a pillar candle, these illuminating shelves are sure to create just the right ambience.

What You Need

- 1 x 6 board, 72 inches (1.8 m) long or 18 inches (45.7 cm) for each shelf
- Ruler
- Pencil
- Handsaw
- Sandpaper
- Drill and drill bits
- Carpenter's glue
- Wood screws
- Acrylic paints
- Paintbrush
- Composition silver leaf (optional)

What You Do

1. Measure and cut one 12-inch (30.5 cm) length of wood for each shelf. This piece is the shelf back. Determine its top and bottom edges.

2. Measure and cut one 6-inch (15.2 cm) length of wood for each shelf. This piece is the shelf ledge. Determine its front and rear ends.

3. Use a handsaw to round the top two corners of the shelf backs for a dramatic curve. If you prefer a less pronounced corner, simply soften the edges with sandpaper. Round the front corners of the shelf ledges in the same manner.

4. Mark a point in the center of the shelf backs, each approximately 1 inch (2.54 cm) below the top edge.

5. Choose a drill bit, and drill a hole at the marked points (the diameter is up to you). A larger hole allows the wall color to peek through as shown in the photo.

6. Place one shelf ledge on the bottom edge of one shelf back. Spread a thin coat of carpenter's glue between the pieces, and then secure the ledge with three wood screws. Repeat this step for each shelf.

7. These shelves are rag-painted to echo the wall treatment of the room. A contrasting white outline boldly silhouettes the shape of each shelf. Alternately, the backs of two shelves are coated with silver composition leaf to softly reflect the glow of the candles. Feel free to apply these enhancement techniques, or finish the shelves as desired.

COLLECTOR SHELVES

A cluster of small shelves produces a dynamic wall focal point. This dramatic effect is easier to achieve than you might think. Select a commercial bracket design, and buy it in bulk. Cut the shelves to fit, and finish both elements to suit the unique style of your room.

What You Need

- Decorative wood shelf brackets (we used six for this project)*
- Tape measure
- 1/2 x 6 new or recycled board, 61 inches (1.5 m) long
- Handsaw
- Sandpaper
- Interior-grade enamel paint, or finish of your choice
- Paintbrush
- Level
- Finishing nails, 1 inch (2.5 cm)
- Hammer
- Nail set
- Wood putty
- Putty knife
- Carpenter's glue

*Purchase decorative wood shelf brackets at any craft or home improvement store. If you'd rather create custom brackets of your own design, simply cut them from pieces of 1/2 x 6 board, and then attach suitable hanging hardware.

What You Do

1. Measure, and then cut the 1/2 x 6 board into six pieces, each 10 inches (25.4 cm) in length. These are the shelf boards. Sand all the edges of the cut wood to the desired shape.

2. Paint the shelf boards and brackets with interior-grade enamel paint, or finish as desired.

3. Determine where to hang the shelves on the wall. Use a level and a pencil to draw both horizontal and vertical hanging guidelines on the wall for the brackets.

4. Fasten each bracket to the wall using the supplied hardware. (If no hardware is supplied, use finishing nails. Nail them in at an angle from the top edge of the bracket and toenail them from the bracket's bottom edge. Use a hammer and nail set to hide the nail heads, fill the holes with wood putty, and let dry. Sand the excess dried putty, and then touch up the paint as needed.)

5. Use a level and a pencil to make horizontal guidelines for the shelves over the top of the brackets. Center and attach the shelves to the top side of the brackets with carpenter's glue and finishing nails. Use a hammer and nail set to hide the nail heads, fill the holes with wood putty, and let dry. Sand the excess dried putty, and then repaint the shelf board as needed.

U SHELF SET

H ere's a simple shelf project with a distinctly modern twist. Construct two elongated U shapes from thick boards and attach them directly to your wall with heavy screws. Use the side pieces as bookends if you wish. They're sturdy enough to support small electronics, and with a coat of crisply colored paint, they also make a strong design statement.

What You Need

- Tape measure
- Handsaw
- 2 x 8 board, 10 feet (3 m) long
- Try square
- Sandpaper
- Level
- 20 nails, 4 inches (10.2 cm)
- Hammer
- Drill and screwdriver bit
- Countersink bit, $3/8$ inch (9.5 mm)
- Lag screws, 4 inches (10.2 cm), $1/2$-inch (1.3 cm) diameter
- Carpenter's glue
- Wood putty
- Putty knife
- Interior-grade enamel paint, in color of your choice
- Paintbrush
- Painter's tape

What You Do

1. Measure and cut two 36-inch (.9 m) lengths from the 2 x 8 board. Cut four additional lengths from the board, each measuring 9 inches (22.9 cm). Check the cut edges for square, and then sand them smooth.

2. Determine the heights at which to hang the shelves. Using a level and a pencil, lightly mark a guideline on the wall at these points. Stack the shelves vertically as shown, or stagger them if desired.

3. Working from the outer edges, use 4-inch (10.2 cm) nails to fasten the horizontal element of the bottom shelf into wall studs. Hammer the nails in at an angle, and hammer their heads flush.

4. Using the drill and the $3/8$-inch (9.5 mm) countersink bit, make pilot holes through the underside of the shelf and into the wall at a 45-degree angle. Drill into studs if possible; otherwise, use heavy-duty hollow-wall fasteners.

5. Use the drill and a screwdriver bit to fasten the shelf to the wall with 4-inch (10.2 cm) lag screws. Countersink the screws into the pilot holes.

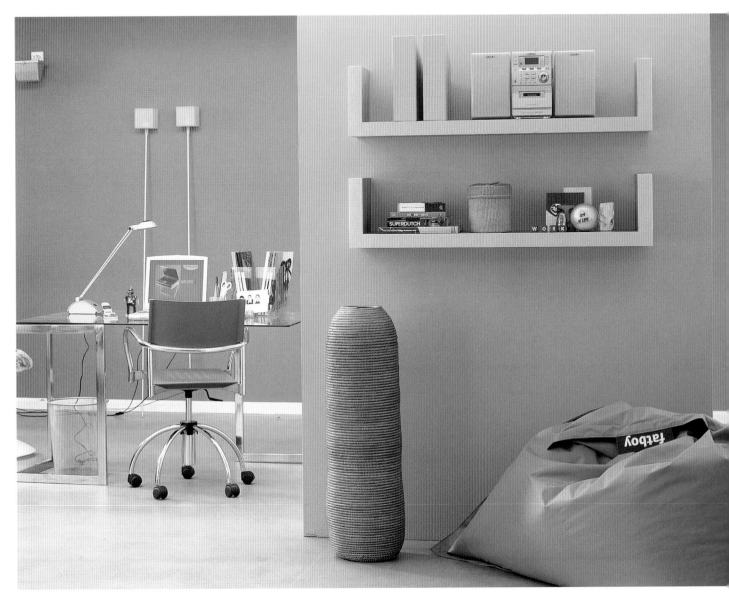

6. Repeat steps 3 through 5 to attach the horizontal element of the top shelf.

7. Use a level and a pencil to lightly mark vertical guidelines for the side pieces of the U shelves.

8. Fasten one side piece to each end of the horizonal shelves using wood glue and lag screws. Check that the shelf elements are square, and adjust as needed.

9. Attach the top of each side piece to the wall with lag screws. Countersink all screws.

10. Use wood putty to fill in the screw holes, allow it to dry, and then sand. Sand the mounted shelves. Mask off the surrounding wall with painter's tape, and then paint the shelves with interior-grade enamel paint or finish as desired.

KITCHEN STATION

B esides looking great, this shelf unit helps you stay organized. Install the shelves and dowel rods at any level. Pick a style of molding or trim that appeals to you, and then paint the whole unit to coordinate with your kitchen.

What You Need

- Tape measure
- Handsaw
- 1 x 6 board, 16 feet (4.9 m)
- Try square
- Carpenter's glue
- 2 bar clamps
- Wood screws, 2 ½ inches (6.4 cm)
- Level
- Dowel rod, 45 inches (1.1 m) long, 1-inch (2.5 cm) diameter
- 4 rod hanger brackets
- Wood screws, 1 inch (2.5 cm)
- Combination square
- Drill with screwdriver attachment and countersinking drill bit
- 2 pieces picture frame molding or decorative trim, each 24 inches (60.9 cm) long
- 2 pieces picture frame molding or decorative trim, each 48 inches (1.2 m) long
- Sandpaper
- Finishing nails, 1 inch (2.5 cm)
- Wood putty
- Putty knife
- Painter's tape
- Interior-grade enamel paint, in color of your choice
- Paintbrush

Note: You may paint the boards prior to constructing the shelf, but the wood-putty-covered nail holes will have to be touched up after installation.

What You Do

1. Measure and cut the 1 x 6 board into four pieces, each 22 inches (55.9 cm) in length. Measure and cut two more pieces of the board, each 48 inches (1.2 m) long. Check all cut corners with the try square, and adjust as needed.

2. Run a bead of carpenter's glue down the ends of two of the 22-inch-long (55.9 cm) wood pieces. Butt their ends together with the ends of the 48-inch-long (1.2 m) pieces to form a 24 x 48-inch (.6 x 1.2 m) box. Hold the box together with clamps, check that it's square, and then fasten the corners with 2 ½-inch (6.4 cm) wood screws.

3. Mark a line that's 12 inches (30.5 cm) down from whichever end you determine to be the top of the box. Run a bead of carpenter's glue on both edges of one of the remaining 22-inch-long (55.9 cm) boards. Install it on the marked line as the workstation's top shelf. Square the position of the shelf, and then attach it with wood screws from the outside edges of the box. Measure 12 inches (30.5 cm) down from the bottom edge of the top shelf, and install the second shelf, following the same process.

4. Determine the positions for the dowel rods. (These will vary according to your individual spacing needs.) Use the level to position the four rod brackets, and then attach them inside the box with 1-inch (2.5 cm) wood screws. Cut two pieces of dowel rod, each 22 inches (55.9 cm) long, and place them into the brackets.

5. Use multiple 2¹/₂-inch (6.4 cm) wood screws to attach the trimless workstation shelf to the wall. Screw through the shelf's bottom, top, and side elements. Install it into studs if possible; otherwise, use hollow-wall fasteners. Countersink all screws to hide their heads.

6. Use a combination square to mark a 45-degree angle on both ends of all four sections of picture frame molding or decorative trim. Point the angle marks toward the center. The outside corners of the molding or trim should measure either 24 inches (60.9 cm) for the horizontal pieces or 48 inches (1.2 m) for the vertical pieces.

7. Use a handsaw to carefully cut along the angle lines marked in step 6. Sand the cut edges of the molding or trim. Use carpenter's glue and clamps to assemble the pieces into a 24 x 48-inch (.6 x 1.2 m) frame. Adjust for square, and then let dry.

8. Attach the frame to the wall-hung unit with 1-inch (2.5 cm) finishing nails. Mask off the wall around the shelf with painter's tape. Sand, and then paint the unit using interior-grade enamel.

PLANTER SHELF

Cut a trio of circles out of a shelf board for a unique planter display. Safe from gusting winds or rambunctious party guests, your special pots of flowers and herbs will flourish in these well-guarded containers.

What You Need

- Tape measure
- Handsaw
- $5/4$ x 8 board, 60 inches (1.5 m)
- Try square
- Combination square
- Twine, 3 to 4 inches (7.6 to 10.2 cm)
- Pencil
- Finishing nails, 1 inch (2.5 cm)
- Drill with countersinking screwdriver attachment
- Drill bit, $1/4$ inch (6 mm)
- Routing drill bit, $3/4$ inch (1.9 cm)
- Jigsaw
- Level
- Wood screws, $2^1/2$ inches (6.4 cm)
- Carpenter's glue
- Wood putty
- Putty knife
- Sandpaper
- Painter's tape
- Exterior-grade enamel paint, in color of your choice
- Paintbrush

Note: You may paint the boards prior to constructing the shelf, but the wood-putty-covered nail holes will have to be touched up after installation.

What You Do

1. Measure and cut one 36-inch (.9 m) length off the $5/4$ x 8 board. Measure and cut two more pieces of board, each 12 inches (30.5 cm) long. Make sure the ends of all three boards are square.

2. Using the combination square, mark a 67 $1/2$-degree angle on one end of each of the 12-inch (30.5 cm) boards. Mark the boards so one end remains 8 inches (20.3 cm), while the second end measures approximately 2 inches (5 cm). Use a handsaw to cut along the marked angles.

3. Tie the twine in a loose knot around the pencil. Tack a finishing nail into the shelf board in the center of the first planter hole. Tie the twine's loose end to the nail so you have about 3 inches (7.6 cm) between the pencil and nail. With the twine taut, run the pencil around the nail to draw a 6-inch (8.5 cm) circle. Repeat this process to mark the additional planter holes.

4. Using the drill and $1/4$-inch (6 mm) bit, drill several pilot holes along the circles so that a jigsaw may be inserted. Use the jigsaw to carefully cut out the marked circles to create the shelf's planter holes.

5. Mark a level horizontal guideline on the wall where you want to hang your shelf. Mount the angled brackets on the wall just below this line using $2^1/2$-inch (6.4 cm) wood screws. Angle in the screws from the top and the bottom of the brackets, and countersink the screw heads.

6. Center the shelf board, check it for level, and then attach it to the brackets, using carpenter's glue and wood screws. Countersink any exposed screw heads, and then fill the holes with wood putty. Allow the putty to dry; then sand.

7. Mask off the surrounding wall, and then paint the planter shelf with exterior-grade enamel paint.

BOARD-MOUNTED SHELF

A coordinated backing board increases a simple shelf's visual impact. Painted a peaceful blue, this shelf installation becomes essential to this room's cohesive image. Build your own shelf to mount following the instructions below, or use a commercial shelf if you wish.

What You Need

- 2 x 4 board, 48 inches (122 cm)
- Tape measure
- Handsaw
- Try square
- Combination square
- Carpenter's glue
- 2 bar clamps
- Finishing nails, 2 inches (5 cm)
- Hammer
- Nail set
- Wood putty
- Putty knife
- Sandpaper
- Mounting board, 34 x 30 x 1 inch (84 x 76.2 x 2.5 cm)
- $5/4$ x 8 board, 30 inches (76.2 cm)
- Wood screws, 2 inches (5 cm)
- Ripsaw
- Painter's tape
- Interior-grade enamel paint, color of your choice
- Paintbrush

Note: You may paint the boards prior to constructing the shelf, but the wood-putty-covered nail holes will have to be touched up after installation.

What You Do

1. Measure and cut two pieces of the 2 x 4 board, each 12 inches (30.5 cm) in length.

2. Measure and cut two pieces of the 2 x 4 board, each $8^{1}/_{4}$ inches (21 cm) in length.

3. Using the tape measure and the try square, draw a line on each of the $8^{1}/_{4}$-inch (21 cm) boards, marking the 8-inch (20.3 cm) point.

4. Set a combination square at a 67 $^{1}/_{2}$-degree angle. On both of the $8^{1}/_{4}$-inch (21 cm) boards, mark a $67^{1}/_{2}$-degree angle line pointing toward the center. Cut one end of each board at this angle.

5. Starting from the square ends of the $8^{1}/_{4}$-inch (21 cm) boards, use a tape measure and try square to mark lines at the 5 $^{1}/_{2}$-inch (14 cm) point.

6. Place a bead of carpenter's glue on each end of the 12-inch (30.5 cm) boards. Butt the ends of these boards with the $8^{1}/_{4}$-inch (21 cm) boards to form a box, using the lines marked at the $5^{1}/_{2}$-inch (14 cm) point as the front of the box.

7. Clamp the box together with two bar clamps, check it for square, and adjust as needed. Use finishing nails to attach the sides to the front and the back of the box.

BUILDING SIMPLE SHELVES

Use a hammer and nail set to countersink the nails. Fill the nail holes with wood putty, let dry, and sand smooth.

8. Mark the level at which you wish to attach the shelf to the backing board. Mark the center of this line. Use wood screws to attach the back of the box to the front of the mounting board in a centered and level position.

9. To make the shelf board, measure and cut an 18-inch (45.7 cm) piece of the $^5/_4 \times 8$ board.

10. To make the brackets, measure and cut a 12-inch (30.5 cm) piece of the $^5/_4 \times 8$ board. Measure and rip-cut this 12-inch (30.5 cm) board into two boards that are each 2$^1/_2$ inches (6.4 cm) wide.

11. Use a tape measure to mark two lines on each of the two brackets. Make each set of lines 8 inches (20.3 cm) apart.

12. At each of the 8-inch (20.3 cm) line marks on the two brackets, use a combination square to mark two parallel 45-degree angles. Cut the ends of the boards on these angles.

13. Apply a bead of carpenter's glue to the ends of the brackets, and clamp them to the inside edges of the box. Make sure the angles are flush with the front inside edge of the box and the mounting board.

14. Attach the brackets to the box with 2-inch (5 cm) wood screws. Toenail the bottom of the bracket to the mounting board with finishing nails. Countersink any visible finishing nails, apply wood putty, let dry, and sand.

15. If needed, use a handsaw to cut off any extra wood from the top of the bracket, before sanding it flush with the top of the box.

16. Center and attach the shelf board to the bracketed box using bar clamps and carpenter's glue.

17. Use a handsaw or sandpaper to trim the points of the top front edges of the box to fit flush with the front edge of the shelf.

18. Determine the location for your shelf, centering the mounting board over at least two wall studs if possible. Attach the mounting board to studs using several wood screws or use hollow-wall fasteners as needed.

19. Use painter's tape to mask off the wall surrounding the shelf. Paint the shelf any color you desire using an interior-grade enamel.

CONTRIBUTING DESIGNERS

Bill Alexander specializes in unique one-of-a-kind handcrafted furnishings created from a variety of found and recycled materials, including barn wood, windows, doors, shutters, and ladders, as well as branches and twigs. His business, From the Mountains to the Sea, is located in Asheville, North Carolina.

Paula Heyes is a talented craftsperson who lives in Asheville, North Carolina, with her husband and two sons.

Joan K. Morris' artistic endeavors have led her down many successful creative paths. A childhood interest in sewing turned into professional costuming for motion pictures. After studying ceramics, Joan ran her own clay windchime business for 15 years. Since 1993, Joan has owned Vincent's Ear, a downtown coffeehouse in Asheville, North Carolina. As a designer for Lark Books, Joan's projects have been featured in *Beautiful Ribbon Crafts* (Spring 2003), *The Weekend Crafter: Dried Flower Crafts* (Spring 2003), *Gifts for Babies* (Spring 2003), Halloween: *A Grown-up's Guide to Creative Costumes, Devilish Decor & Fabulous Festivities* (Fall 2003), *Hardware Style* (Fall 2003), and *Creating Fantastic Vases* (Fall 2003).

Terry Taylor is the principle in-house craft designer for Lark Books. Projects from Terry's abundant and resourceful imagination are featured in many Lark publications, in addition to the books he writes and edits, such as *The Weekend Crafter: Paper Crafting* (Spring 2003) and *Creative Candlescaping* (Fall 2004). In his life outside of Lark, Terry is a well-respected multimedia artist and jeweler.

DESIGNER INDEX

ACKNOWLEDGMENTS

Many thanks to all the people who contributed to this book, including Bill Alexander, Hannes Charen, Dawn Cusick, Paige Gilchrist, Delores Gosnell, Paula Heyes, Dana Irwin, Megan Kirby, Deborah Morgenthal, Nathalie Mornu, Joan K. Morris, Rick Morris, Rob Pulleyn, Pete Roberts, Terry Taylor, Derrick Tickle, Shannon Yokeley, and Barbara Zaretsky.

Barbara Zaretsky's beautiful wearable textile art is featured on page 40. Please visit her website: http://home.earthlink.net/~bzfish/

Derick Tickle's appealing hand-painted furniture appears on pages 42 and 89.

INDEX

NOTES ABOUT SUPPLIERS

Usually, the supplies you need for making the projects in Lark books can be found at your local craft supply store, discount mart, home improvement center, or retail shop relevant to the topic of the book. Occasionally, however, you may need to buy materials or tools from specialty suppliers. In order to provide you with the most up-to-date information, we have created a listing of suppliers on our website, which we update on a regular basis. Visit us at www.larkbooks.com; click on "Craft Supply Sources"; and then click on the relevant topic. You will find numerous companies listed with their website address and/or mailing address and phone number.